IS YOUR BOSS MAD?

The definitive
guide to
coping with
your boss

Jill Walker

Crown House Publishing Ltd
www.crownhouse.co.uk
www.chpus.com

First published by

Crown House Publishing Ltd
Crown Buildings, Bancyfelin, Carmarthen, Wales, SA33 5ND, UK
www.crownhouse.co.uk

and

Crown House Publishing Company LLC
6 Trowbridge Drive, Suite 5, Bethel, CT 06801, USA
www.chpus.com

First published 2007. Reprinted 2007.

British Library of Cataloguing-in-Publication Data
A catalogue entry for this book is available
from the British Library.

10-digit ISBN 184590039-1
13-digit ISBN 978-184590039-7

LCCN 2006932136

Printed and bound in the UK by
Cromwell Press, Trowbridge, Wiltshire

Mixed Sources
Product group from well-managed
forests and other controlled sources
www.fsc.org Cert no. TT-TOC-2082
© 1996 Forest Stewardship Council

Contents

Preface

This book is not aimed at work-shy, soap dodging, unambitious couch potatoes. I have assumed at least that you: (a) need to be employed, and (b) believe that the swapping of time for money, which constitutes the basis for 'employment', sit with you as a fair exchange. I am taking it for granted that you are interested in progressing your career, and that in some way, however basic or however complex, you bring certain skills to your workplace. Top of the list is the belief that you have the self-respect of wanting to do your job as well as you can.

What this book isn't

This is not a smart-arse book that will help you trick your employers. Neither is this a 'get out of stuff' or 'how to get even' manifesto. It is not meant to help you sue your boss for situations that you manipulate, nor is it to make other people miserable. And in no way is this merely an exquisite example of negative thinking!

What this book is

This book is designed to put you in a positive state of mind for dealing with the wickedness that can manifest as an inevitable consequence of working for someone else. As an 'employee' you cannot just do what you want; you have to heed the wishes of others, and at times you will interpret these wishes as evidence of madness, or badness, or sheer incompetence. However, that person is probably getting paid more than you, has more clout than you, and unfortunately may have the power to relieve you of your position. These poor bosses will make the mistake of imagining there are plenty more where you came from.

It is a plain guide for coping in the face of madness – from others, and from your own madness if things are getting too much. To do this, you need strategies, and this book will give you practicable strategies.

Your success with these strategies will ensue if the following 'hygiene factors' are followed 100%. For example:

1. You turn up for work, on time (special, unplanned, emergency situations excluded) and are dressed appropriately.

2. You are not verbally or physically abusive.

3. You have established that you are qualified for the job as described in the hiring process.

I would like to say your skills should match the 'job description', but sadly such documents are not always available at the interview. Try requesting it! That is likely to be viewed positively and will help them make a decision about whether or not to hire you! If a job description does not exist, then offer to write it when you have been in the role for a while.

What the book has to offer

I am going to describe nine different profiles of mad bosses – the 'pure types'. However, when you are dealing with real people, you often find a mixture of behaviours. Therefore, where appropriate, I'll indicate how these pure types are typically combined in real characters. I describe these in chapters four to twelve.

The first type is the *Friend Then Foe Then Friend Again* boss. You will probably recognise his moodiness and inconsistent behaviour. I then explore the world of the *Mr Long Hours* boss who thinks that working all the hours of the day is a desirable trait. I next look into how power corrupts in the *Power Crazy* and *No Power* boss profiles.

If you have ever worked for someone who seemed to resent your existence then you will appreciate the *I Hired You, Now I Hate You* boss. Then I reveal what it's really like working in sales, and how if you wish to stay sane in the mad world of the *Sales Manager* boss, it will require a great deal of resilience on your part.

You will find out about the differences between power corrupted bosses and those who manage with fear in the *Fear Merchant*. These mad bosses, like the *Small Business Owner* boss, are experts at creating and controlling their own immediate little world. And if all that is not enough to cope with at work, you may even have to endure the romantic attention of your boss, which is covered in the *Boss In Love*.

And then there are chapters which are more generally useful.

■ The interview scenario; use it to ask more than just about the company growth strategy

◆ Interview techniques to be aware of

■ Stress and the organisations that advise you …

■ Fun Stuff – bring fun to work

■ Saying Goodbye

Acknowledgments

Of course, I would like to be able to thank all the people who influenced and inspired me to write this book, however, given the circumstances I think that may not be appropriate! But I thank you all anyway, very, very much …

I would like to thank Caroline Lenton of Crown House for her faith in me. I am very grateful for Caroline's generous support and guidance and her refreshing and positive attitude to this project. I would also like to thank my editor Peter Young and his patience with me. Peter, a tough task master, kept my feet on the ground. His challenges to my work have added clarity to my arguments, thank you Peter.

I would like to thank my wonderful daughters, Lauren, Naomi, Olivia, and Rianna for their patience with a mother with whom they had to share this work, this new baby, for many months. Thank you, my lovely girls.

Thanks also to the many people who told me their tales of their work experience, explaining the details of their mad boss, and how they coped, you may see your story here.

Is Your Boss Mad?

'Successful business managers may share many of their personality traits with those found among incarcerated patients legally classified as having psychopathic disorder or mental illness.

Belinda Board and Katarina Fritzon (University of Surrey) found that a sample of senior British managers and chief executives averaged higher scores on self-reported measures of histrionic, narcissistic, and compulsive personality than did two samples of former and current patients at Broadmoor hospital.

These personality dimensions reflect characteristics such as superficial charm, lack of empathy and perfectionism. However, unlike the Broadmoor patients, the business managers scored significantly lower on antisocial, borderline, and paranoid personality dimensions.

These dimensions reflect characteristics such as aggression, impulsivity, and mistrust. "The senior business managers appear to possess ... elements of psychopathic personality disorder that have been referred to as the emotional components, and they closely resemble characteristics known to be beneficial to achieving in a senior management role", the authors said. These findings are consistent with the concept of 'successful psychopaths' – "people with personality disorder patterns, but without the characteristic history of arrest and incarceration", they explained.

Board and Fritzon's results were obtained by asking 39 business managers to complete the Minnesota Multiphasic Inventory for DSM III Personality Disorders, and by comparing their scores with those recorded for 1,085 current and former patients at Broadmoor. "The relatively small sample size of the business manager sample calls into question the reliability of these results", the authors cautioned.'

Board, B.J. & Fritzon, Katarina, F. (2005). **Disordered personalities at work.** Psychology, Crime and Law, 11, 17-32.

A Company ...

'A company is like a tree full of monkeys. The ones at the top look down and all they see is lots of happy faces smiling up at them. The monkeys down below look up into the branches above and all they can see are arseholes ...'

Introduction

The alarm clock rings loudly, your heart jumps; can it really be morning already? It feels like only a minute since your head hit the pillow. The dawn of a new day has arrived! You roll over in bed with the sound still ringing in your ears! And you lie there thinking, "I have to get up! Another day, another dollar." But just like yesterday, and probably tomorrow, you are not leaping out of bed, full of joy, nor looking forward to the new day with all its challenges and satisfying effort. Of course, you could easily claim that we would all rather not work at all, but the hard reality is that most of us have to work, and most of us don't enjoy it as much as we would like.

These are the days of your life. Every moment is precious. You must decide: are you going to rerun the bitter twisted memories of your so-called working life, focusing on the regrets and wishing you had had the guts to do something different; or are you going to bask in the happy memories of days spent in satisfying, productive toil, knowing that was a job well done?

You may not have realised that you have that choice. However things turn out, remember that in some way you are always in a position where you do have some power to make choices, even if that choice is to walk away. It may come to that, but first you need to be aware of the other options available.

What changed?

Once upon a time you attended a great interview. Suddenly the future offered you a glimpse of some of its richness, and you were only too eager to get going. And then … The interesting question is: what happens between that initial enthusiastic, "I want to do a good job! Be successful", and the steady decline into despondency when your plans do not work out as expected (tip: they never do) and your work becomes the place you dread, so much so that you will do almost anything to avoid it? How does 'an opportunity to work with a great team' so often turn into a coronary-inducing scenario? What shift in the universe turns you from being a happy weekend person into a grizzly, unhappy weekday, work-mode person?

Can you imagine a world where work *is* satisfying? Where you feel valued and feel you want to give your employer your total loyalty? Maybe you did once? So what happened to erode that desire?

What makes the difference between the workplace you dread and the workplace you enjoy? To a certain extent, it is the company processes, possibly decided by distant decision-makers who may or may not have a total grasp of life 'at the coalface' that dictate your experience. The rules that govern your work-life can crush the creativity and personality you want to bring to your role in order to serve the requirements of the greater organisation. But it's not just the place or the processes, it's the people you work with who govern the mood of the workplace. And above all, it is that particular person who manages you, your BOSS, who exerts the greatest influence. Without doubt, the personality and behaviour of your boss carries the greatest impact on whether you enjoy your work or not.

The simple solution to solving this problem

I always advocate that every person involved in people management needs training. However, training is only the first step; it can help, but it does not ensure good management. As employees, we are still at the mercy of managers who can be abusive, bullying, sarcastic, aggressive, ineffectual or lazy. So another solution – one which you can be actively involved in yourself – is to find ways of learning how to deal with such bosses, who are there in great numbers in the real world of employment. What you need is a guide, which offers the help, the strategies and the tools you need to cope with managers, both trained and untrained.

It may seem obvious that your boss is a human being … but sometimes it is easy to forget! Bosses arrive at the workplace, more through luck than judgment, carrying, just like the rest of us, a huge invisible sack slung heavily over their multi-chipped shoulder, containing their bruised egos, paranoia and complicated neuroses. In addition, bosses carry with them the burden of having to live up to what we expect from them. This is the disconnect that we will be exploring. One place to start is to understand what motivates and drives your boss, and which human frailties they bring to work. Once you can recognise these factors, you are in a position to start to take action.

Unfortunately, bosses do not come with a user's manual. You have to work it out for yourself: "Why does he make such strange requests? How come I can't predict what mood she will be in today? How can I tell if he has a sense of humour? Why does she think I will perform under this amount of pressure? Why doesn't he understand me? Why doesn't she help me? Why can't I talk to him? Why can't things be more friendly…?"

This book seeks to examine the behaviour of nine kinds of bosses, through case studies, and in doing so create profiles. Some of these profiles may be familiar to you; they are all types that cause misery in the workplace. They are based on true stories recounted by friends, family, and colleagues. But don't pay too much attention to the different companies or environments in which they are set; it is more important to recognise the profiles. (I have deliberately not enhanced the details of the companies or organisations involved.)

This is not a book about the particular personalities of some bosses, but a guide that will help you recognise generalities and deeper patterns, and how personal pressures, fears and drivers influence the 'mad' behaviour of bosses.

These case studies come not just from my personal experience of having bad bosses, but also from my headhunting and recruitment days. Sadly, working with many managers as candidates, I developed a healthy lack of respect for those people who called themselves 'bosses' – but a real appreciation of the good ones. The experience also taught me to be comfortable talking to anyone regardless of seniority, and confident enough to ask and probe them with what, on the surface, could have appeared inappropriate questions. It now seems second nature for me to ask about topics such as family and hobbies. Some people would think these are not necessarily the things one 'should' ask when meeting a business leader or boss, but they start to give you insight into the personality behind the title.

As with any kind of typology, few are pure types, most are mixtures. As your particular boss is almost certainly a combination of profiles, I will describe the range. This will help you sort out who you are dealing with, as this will be useful when creating your strategies. Having identified the profile(s) of your boss, I shall explore some of the possible causes of the particular traits they are exhibiting, and suggest some suitable strategies for coping for each profile. These strategies are designed to help you manage your workplace environment to your advantage and generally improve how you manage your working life.

Fluffy gurus

You have probably read or come across management books that talk in abstract terms, describing leadership or management styles, training methods and complicated methodology. Those books all assume that you are dealing with rational human beings. This book is different. It does not refer to lofty ideals that in our real world are beyond the reach or comprehension of your average boss (sadly the majority are average) or employee; instead, it deals with nuts-and-bolts tactics for coping. To help you manage your working situation, there are detailed instructions, and even, in some cases, the appropriate language forms to use. This isn't an 'ideal world' theory manual; it throws a line down into the mire so that you can drag yourself out!

Above all else, remember that you are not alone. By sharing in the experiences of the people mentioned in this book you will realise the world is full of mad bosses and that it is possible to work for one and still have a life. With my help, you should be able to evolve a strategy to cope with or even improve your situation. Once you begin to understand why you have found yourself (or constantly find yourself) in a difficult, uncomfortable or unhappy work situation, you will be able to cope with things so much better. Once you are taking responsibility and behaving proactively, rather than playing victim, you will experience an immediate level of relief. I want you to enjoy your job, to be free of tension, and to be a part of helping your workplace become a happier environment.

Yes, it is possible to have harmony in your workplace, and it is possible for you to implement ways of creating the changes you would like, or at least start the process towards achieving them. And that means that one day you will look back at your working life, and smile …

Chapter One
The World of Work

I wish I'd spent more time at the office ...

The epitaph no one wants on their tombstone.

Throughout my working life, the roles I have enjoyed most were those where, because I have had a good working relationship with my boss, I had access to the pressures and challenges that the company was facing. When you understand what the organisation is up against, when you can talk to your boss and offer helpful suggestions, you feel valued and develop an empathy for their situation. But those situations were relatively rare, and whenever the boss was 'closed' to discussing the wider company problems, I invariably felt frustrated. I am sure that this refusal or inability to share their mindset has been the cause of many an employee's experience of a mad boss.

It was when I took on a recruitment and headhunting role that I gained many more insights into how bosses think. I developed the confidence to talk to them in their language, and to see things from their point of view. But not all the candidates were managers. On more than one occasion during the years I spent as a recruitment consultant, I found myself listening to drained candidates at the end of their tether, asking for my help to get them away from utterly miserable employment situations. It is their experiences that are discussed here – in addition to those of my family and friends.

My primary activity at that time was to place very senior people, including managing directors, chief executive officers, country and regional managers, sales directors and sales managers in new positions. It was always an exciting moment to finally get to speak to the man I was after, and to see his CV in all its glory before me!

Hey, just look at this guy! He speaks three languages, has ten years in the industry and is working for a market leader! What a find – it will be great to place him! Senior, experienced, educated, and interested in looking for a new role. Perfect!

I'd get mentally prepared, have all the details to hand, and call him, "Is that Mr X?" By way of an answer would come a thin, nervous little voice, "Hello", and a wave of disappointment would sweep over me:

> Can the person answering my call really be the god described on the CV that I was holding with anticipation in my trembling hand just a moment ago? Perhaps I shouldn't really go on the sound of his voice … but honestly, he doesn't sound up to much.

And from that point on it would all be downhill.

The process of placing a candidate reveals too much. In the course of several weeks you find out what they earn, what they aspire to, what they fear. You know about the details of their work history, including the details of where things 'went wrong'. You learn about the places where there were 'personality clashes', the companies they had to leave before they had 'a chance to prove themselves'.

Finding that perfect new role is a process that means a lot of time is spent talking through personal issues: where they want to live, which schools they want their kids to attend, personal details about their wife, husband, partner, dog … all the normal minutiae of life is laid bare.

A candidate's ego is revealed in the questions they ask. And when it comes to ego, size really does matter. Some candidates struggle with the scope and responsibility of the job. Acceptable roles are selected not just on the basis of the salary, but in terms of status. The questions asked are: "Who will I report to?" "What will my title be?" "What car goes with the job?" "How many people will report to me?" Of course, there is nothing wrong with these questions; they are part of understanding the role. But as they were discussed, I began to get a view of the real man or woman, the real manager behind the CV. And at this point, I would start to wonder: What are they really worried about? What are the drivers behind the personality? How will these affect their success in a new role?

Fears about failure, pressures from other areas of their life, their hopes and weaknesses, their neurosis – I was privy to them all. They worried about their age, their weight, and about going bald! Over time I became less and less impressed with candidates simply because they revealed too much of themselves, and all I could see was their common humanity.

My thoughts would continue: "How will these worries manifest in the candidate's new role?" I knew I would never see the people I placed in action, but I did start to notice patterns in the personality types, regularities in their work paths, in their behaviour, and even in the type of speech they used. On this basis, I was able to notice differences between the truly great managers and the far more common, average ones.

I am sure these bosses made a great impression on day one of their new jobs: arriving in their new, leather upholstered cars, clad in fine new suits, crisp white shirts, tasteful ties. They were sure to 'cut it' in front of their new employees. They would absolutely go on to make superb strategic decisions and start rolling out policies that would improve their new companies no end. But I would always wonder at what stage their personality traits would cut in, at what point their means of disguising their weaknesses and fears would fail.

This experience of being very 'intimate' with a lot of very senior leaders enabled me to see beyond the 'public self' behaviours that manifest at interview, to those which are lying hidden, waiting to emerge in all their glory when dealing with innocent employees! Have no doubt; every boss brings a mixture of insecurities and fears along to complement their management style. This book examines and explains the drivers of their decisions, their behaviours, and their moods.

There are any number of ways for describing personality (and many big businesses earning fortunes at profiling), so to keep things manageable, I am going to identify nine typical nightmare boss profiles. Some of the characteristics and behaviours you will recognise in your boss. Now you'll understand *why* they are aggressive, defensive, lazy, or moody – and learn how best to communicate with them.

So when you hear that alarm clock, I want you to have a different response. I'd like you to get up willingly and enthusiastically, and really looking forward to going to work. With all these insights into what's really going on in your work environment, you'll be able to work towards creating an atmosphere in which work is a pleasure, and in which working with the boss is mutually satisfying.

Discrimination

This is not a legal publication. If you feel you have grounds for unfair dismissal, or have been discriminated against on grounds of age, race, sex, religion, and so on, then see a lawyer. Additionally I have not sought to explore sexual harassment in any depth as the work experience in this book is dealt with at a very much more general level. I, like many other women, have experienced it in varying degrees. Within the advice of this book, I explore how you can try to avoid it: the signs to read and some actions that can be taken. But in essence, as with all forms of bullying – don't accept it!

People are in misery the world over – and I'm not talking about hunger, homelessness, or war. It's a work thing. Millions of people are stressed, bullied and dread the prospect of going to work. It's not because they are lazy, it's not because they are stupid, it's because they face an environment that causes them deep anxiety. They are the victims of bosses, supervisors, managers and team leaders who have achieved that position through no more planning than if they had picked a lottery ticket.

I believe this situation has to change. The minimum requirement has to be training for 'people in charge of people', whatever their level, and as an ongoing part of the job. In the meantime, the first action may be to give yourself some time. It is no wonder that 'sickies' can now be seen to have a serious economic impact, and a good indicator of working conditions across different countries. How many sick days does the average worker take off? Why do they do it? Because they need some balance in their lives, and, as a desperate measure, this seems like one way of coping. For many people, chucking it all in is not an option; but the alternative, the more common reality of having a continuous low-level of sickness rather than being well and happy is also not acceptable.

Consider how much time you spend with colleagues at your place of work. Perhaps more waking hours than you generally spend with your partner or family! If your time at work could be enjoyable (or at least tolerable), where you might feel valued and supported, would it change your perspective on work? Could work be fun for the employee as well as efficient and profitable for the employer?

How do you change your perspective? Essentially, the first thing to do is remove yourself from the intolerable situation – and that may mean throwing a sickie. Only by stepping back, by physically getting distance on the situation, can you become objective and learn how to make it work for you.

For bosses, training is available. Many will have completed a course of some description or another. But as you know, simply going on a course is not enough. Human personalities are usually resistant to change, and bosses need to be highly motivated if they are to implement any training they have received. Many undertake the training but are not able to carry it through to the workplace. Listing it on their CV as just another course attended is about the limit. Even then, despite the level of their training, most bosses quickly slip back to exerting control in the ingrained style demanded by their over-riding drivers. Whether from fear, laziness, anxiety, or other type of neurosis, their old style will seep through to the surface in the boss/employee scenario they inhabit. Personality – and inertia – can so easily prevail over the effect of training courses.

There are big challenges ahead. Barring the sudden rush of numerous enlightened, fully trained, inspiring managers and bosses hitting the world-wide workplace, this volume will useful. It will seek to help you take some control back into your work life, and through that control, enjoy it as you and the rest of the world's work-force deserve.

What is your boss like?

Don't tell me: your boss is serene, constantly approachable, a professional calm leader. A person who lights up your work environment, a mentor, someone you admire, aspire to be like, and from whom you learn. Someone you can rely on, who understands you and the challenges and frustrations you have in doing your job. Always ready with an encouraging word or a little joke. A fair, firm, and dazzling communicator; groomed, poised and truly worthy of their position; you can't wait to see them and hope that you will get the chance to discuss a particular work issue that has arisen. Is this your boss?

No! Let's get real. They drive you crazy, and really, deep down, you think they are mad!

How come this seems to be an almost universal syndrome? You turn up at work and find yourself in a situation where the person to whom you will be answerable for the next four, six, eight hours – or more – behaves like a recently escaped inmate from a public institution.

Think back to the heady days of your interview. When the company mission statement was revealed to you, you tingled with excitement at the prospect of being with such an enlightened organisation. This was it; the boss is a rational human being, he has plans, he is organised, he has picked me! I can tell I will be here for years and years! Fantastic!

And then you started work …

I have had extensive first-hand experience of this strange syndrome. The amazing experience of a new job! It's not uncommon for this new position you have committed to stay with, to turn completely sour – amazingly quickly, even in only days or weeks. You find yourself tied to a place where it is possible for the behaviour, attitude, and mood of just a handful of individuals to bring a life of misery to so many. Too late, you realise that the interview presented an opportunity that now bears little or no resemblance to the experience you are actually having. "You will be part of a great team," you distinctly remember them saying. Well, no. The reality of the situation is more, "I am part of a group of equally miserable people."

The skill requirement may have been accurate, the payslip may reflect the agreed remuneration, but things are not right, not happy. Communication with the boss is difficult. You ask questions, but you also need the real answers. You may be finding it difficult to judge their strange behaviour. Maybe they are friendly but completely ineffectual, allowing other elements in your environment to get in the way and stop you from doing what needs to be done. They let you down – failing to deliver and failing to be boss-like. The promises of the interview or hiring process have long been forgotten, your expectations are unfulfilled; the picture you now have is not the picture you were sold.

With this goes the feeling that you just don't want to do the job. Clouds hang over your life: bullying, mood swings, petulance, aggression, and sarcasm emanate from the person to whom, possibly only a few days or weeks before, you committed a significant proportion of your life.

Why can't work be more fun? Why has the person who interviewed you with such attention manifested as the petty tyrant who now stands whining before you? Are companies who cite 'a focus on work-life balance' only paying lip service to entice us poor employees into their particular asylum?

So here's the acid test. In your particular organisation, is there a palpable sigh of relief when the boss is absent? Does the thought of a day at work without your boss mean you sleep better, get up earlier, and feel calmer and happier? Moreover, conversely, does the thought of having to be in close proximity to your boss on a particular day fill you with panic, anxiety, and depression?

So admit it: this is not how it's supposed to be. What can you do? Leave? Go sick? Go onto medication? Kill the boss? There may be another way ...

Chapter Two
What is a Boss?

The boss may be the CEO of the company or the managing director of a business – but for the purposes of this book, the boss is that person who tells you what to do and maybe how to do it. The boss is the person you report to, who is monitoring your performance, checking you arrive on time and don't leave too early. They may have the title 'manager', 'supervisor', 'regional director', 'team leader', or any one of a number of titles. All of which indicate a requirement for some activity involving people management – your management, your boss.

I have worked for men and women and I would state that the traits and behaviours described in this book are definitely not gender specific. It is just for simplicity that unless specifically 'women' related stories, all the bosses referred to in this volume are named 'men' or 'he', but as I say, it's just for convenience. Just for the record, I am no shrinking violet. I have been the only female member of several sales teams which has meant having to be a little tough. It was part of a strategy I had to develop to survive in a man's world.

To be perfectly honest, I have worked for mad female bosses as well, so please accept that the scenarios in the book are not based on sexual categorisation – the traits explored apply equally to male and female bosses.

Most bosses generally have the wrong slant on the reason for their existence. (I have only experienced one who truly understood the rule.) Contrary to popular belief, managers and bosses are not there to discipline you, tell you off, or check your punctuality, but are in fact there to support you and facilitate your success. They are there to make sure you have the tools, resources, environment, training, and qualifications to do your job. They are there to serve you, not the other way round.

They are there to enable you to provide the services the company has employed you for, and fulfil every requirement the business has of you. Their role is to communicate the requirements of the business – and the consequences should you fail to deliver. This is a universal rule: whatever your job – be it a sales or a technical role, whether you are a nurse, or a cleaner – your boss is there to help you, not to make your life difficult. They are there to serve you and provide all the help you need to fulfil your role successfully.

Given the route many bosses have taken to arrive at their boss position, it is, sadly, not unusual for them to totally fail to grasp that concept. They find themselves in their new role completely lacking in the skills necessary for carrying out the proper function. Many will not have received training, but may have been successful in the role they held before 'promotion'. But that does not introduce them to their primary function, that is, to serve their 'subordinates'. Instead, they really believe that they are there to 'tell you what to do'. The fail to learn that only through your success will they ensure their own.

Discipline

An organisation needs discipline, but the discipline has to come from within. The wrong kind of discipline is that used against the employee. That way of applying discipline is not the primary function of a boss, but a consequence of a member of staff failing to deliver. The reason for the failure may not be effectively explored if it reflects badly on the boss's behaviour. It is easier to blame it on a 'general deterioration in communication' or the employee's rejection of wanting to work, rather than on the fact that the employee's self-esteem and confidence has been undermined by a thoughtless boss. In any case, one common result is the breakdown of the relationship.

OK, so bad things happen and the boss needs to take action. But any communication which involves advising the employee of their failure to deliver should either not be delivered at all (a tough one, having to focus on the positive!), or said without sarcasm, aggression, or anger (also tough). In an ideal world, it would not surprise an employee if they were to receive a warning, as it would be the outcome of a recognised company process. For example, if you fail to arrive for work three days in a row without an explanation for your absence, expect a few questions! In this kind of 'warning' conversation the boss would tell the employee about their failure, and subsequent warnings will advise as to when it may mean dismissal or other punishment.

So hang on! Hell! Let's get real! Who are we trying to kid? This situation rarely ever passes without raised voices and swearing. The political correctness book goes straight out the window, sometimes followed by items of furniture! Why do I highlight this at such an early stage? To illustrate the fact that even with all the management training in the world, education or experience, bosses are still human. Yes, they are! Disciplining an employee is just an example of a typical scenario where bosses, who may not have been trained, allow the situation to degenerate into an emotional screaming match, or even a physical punch-up. Such mishandled interventions make things worse. Check your own experience: how often has a boss become emotional, even abusive with you? So what triggered that initial anger? Where did the real responsibility lie? Sometimes anger is reasonable and used to make a point. But more often, it reflects an underlying, unresolved dis-ease within the angry person – which is in no way going to be resolved in a shouting match. Overall, if you only do your job because you are frightened of having someone shout at you, there is a serious problem.

Assume that your boss is motivated, just as you are, but is failing when it comes to controlling the impact of their emotional baggage of fears – their personal drivers in the workplace. A sales director, under pressure because of 'poor figures' and nursing a hangover, can exhibit all the behaviour traits of a two-year-old toddler whose mother has just put his comfort blanket in the wash.

Once you understand these issues, you will know how to deal with them. Of course, the best option may be to ensure that nothing unpleasant happens. If, however, confrontations are unavoidable, and from the boss's point of view, necessary, then you need to know how to use the boss's weaknesses to contain situations. Starting with yourself. Remember that you are going to become more skilled in being in control, because you are maintaining a healthy perspective on events and training yourself to learn and improve. So no longer will you be reacting in the way the boss expects. You will be gently exercising your real power and communicating with ease. Using more subtle techniques of speech and behaviour will smooth your day and make interaction more pleasant and effective. And that includes getting inside the boss's mind (a place you may have previously dreaded going!) in order to get some idea of what goes on, and how that manifests in the behaviours you are familiar with. You will need some tools and techniques to do this, but they are easy to learn, and will pay dividends when it comes to effective communication. You may find that you can get closer to the boss, even tell them about their weak points, and sow the seeds for their improvement.

Why don't you just leave?

Before continuing, let's just check. If it's really so bad, why haven't you already left? Why are you still here if you hate it so much? Why don't you just leave? You are a good, hard worker; you have some great skills. Why not find a new employer, one who deserves your commitment? You may well decide that leaving is the answer. Think about this: if you do decide to leave, jump when you are ready; don't get pushed. Never let a work situation control your decision. (Later we will consider the benefits of being able to control your temper and learning to enjoy the amazing feelings of superiority it can bring.)

As your boss slowly loses the plot and you are able to stand looking calmly on, the feeling of power wells up in you. But use this power wisely. This is not the time to show your anger or tell a few home truths. Nor should you have to take the boss's angry outpourings personally. The more you control yourself, the more you will be in control of the situation. When you decide to leave this job, this role, you will do it when you decide, not when someone else has dictated. Don't leave just because you are so miserable you can't take any more; that is not the time for slamming doors behind you.

Never just walk out. Take your time, because with your new insight into boss and management behaviours, you need time to find the right boss and a role that is sustainable, where you will be able to work with people who value and understand you. You are going to make a positive decision to move towards what you want, rather than run away, however tempting it might seem. Use the techniques in this book to cope through to the moment when you can leave – sweet moment indeed!

On a more practical note, you may well benefit from a reference for your new role. If there is a danger of losing your cool, any inappropriate behaviour could damage your reference. Also, you probably need to practise dealing with mad bosses in a place where you can leave your 'mistakes' behind. If you are going to change the way you react to bullying, aggression or paranoia, start straight away in relatively safe situations. You may even end up deciding not to leave your job. But at least you are making that choice. One of the worst things you can experience in life is a lack of choices. The more you practise thinking in a different way, the more choices will open up for you immediately.

If you have only been in a post for a short while, you may be unwilling to go through the job-changing process so soon, with all the stress that the interview scenario can bring. Again, take the opportunity to use the tools and techniques that will improve your personal power.

As you realise the true breadth of your choices, you will also become aware of the consequences. For the most part, they will be positive and give you the confidence to go on and make your future employment decisions.

Confidence

Think carefully when you are about to implement a strategy. Initially it may slightly raise your stress levels, but this will be a different kind of stress, more like excitement. Not all stress is negative. The excitement or stress you may feel now will be because you are doing something about your situation, and are no longer the bystander in the scene. Don't confuse these emotions with the old feelings of stress you have historically felt.

The basis of many of the strategies depends on you exercising your confidence. This is not always easy, especially if you are anxious about losing your job (at least before you are planning to), or are just afraid of your mad boss. Self-confidence is like a muscle: the more it's used the stronger it gets. So be patient with yourself; be caring with yourself. If you don't feel that you are the world's most confident person, start small and grow your confidence from small successes. Many of the strategies begin by building upon minor actions or interventions which will have positive outcomes, thus allowing your confidence to grow.

As you learn to recognise the mad boss and his tactics, it will help you as you go forward in your career. You will identify the types more quickly, maybe even at the interview stage, and be able to decide at that point whether you wish to proceed. That could save you weeks of stress because either that option will be closed, or if you do accept the job, then at least you will have the know-how for dealing with the mad boss. You may, indeed, relish the challenge, knowing that your progress in the new role will only highlight you in a positive light. To use a slightly corny expression, you will be in a state of mind to shout, about any new role, "Bring it on!"

Managers and team leaders can arrive with no more skill than the next man, put in charge for no other reason other than they raised their hand quicker than their neighbour, but putting them in a position to make so many lives a workplace hell. I know this is how it happens; it happened to me.

Are you a boss?

Boss of the mad boss, ask yourself: How many sick days have your poor managers caused? How much is your mad management costing you? How and why does your organisation promote managers?

If I was running an organisation with any sort of reporting structure, where any person was managed by another, I would want to know if any of those managers were creating an unhappy workplace. I'd want to know if they were causing my business to lose money through absent employees, (re-)hiring costs or by failing to attract the best staff.

An old colleague told me about a company that employed about 75 people, which had 65% staff turnover in one year. This was in the context of the even poorer figure of 300% staff turnover in two years. They had additionally employed three human resources managers in nine months! The cost of hiring and firing these extraordinary numbers must have impacted profits. Have the board members investigated the long-serving (loyal and faithful, or simply poor, aggressive, or ineffectual?) managers remaining and wondered 'Why?'

Many business gurus confirm that if you take advantage of your employees then they will communicate this to your customers and take advantage of them. Fact: unhappy employees give you unhappy customers, damage the business, and impact badly on profits. Recognise the link.

Who gets promoted to boss?

At the interview, did you ever think to ask the question: "So, why did they make you the boss?" Probably not, I would guess. I have heard people ask about, "Where are you from?" (which company) or "What is your background?" (which school or college), but it seems 'impolite' to ask people why they think they have been promoted to their boss role.

At your next interview, make sure you try to find out about the career path of your potential new boss. You can ask it gently: "What qualities do you feel meant that you were highlighted for promotion?" How the boss responds will depend on the sort of personality you start to uncover during the interview. Bear in mind that if the boss is 'prickly' about the question and becomes defensive, they may be exhibiting traits of 'the mad boss', so it is worth finding this out.

Some bosses simply arrived through just being 'available'. If so, don't be surprised if they are not the most innovative people with whom you get to work. However, their 'availability' may reflect a great competence in their original role, which will make them a worthy role model for those skills, and from whom you can learn.

A brief diversion: think about how you have received any promotion in the past, or how your friends and family have been made bosses. What are you like to work for? And what do you think they would be like to work for? I would guess that there may be inklings that an element of 'the mad boss' is present, even in these people you know so well! There are many ways to arrive at a point in your career when you become a manager. These routes, as you can see from the people you know, do not necessarily ensure the skills required to do it well.

Back to your own boss: Why are they in that role? There are several scenarios. Some have been the business owner, others have just been in the
right place at the right time, but sadly most of the rest have just shown
very good results in one discipline – they were the top sales person, or had
good customer service results. Their limited talents catch the attention of
their bosses and they find themselves promoted, as a reward! But that does
not mean that they get the training to go with it, and they suddenly find
themselves out of their depth, and relying on outmoded techniques rather
than having real and appropriate people-management skills.

"So why are you the MD?"

"Because I was the top sales person for the region."

Oh dear …

Are the boss's bosses mad too? Why are people who are successful in sales
so often promoted to a management role? The words 'lamb' and 'slaugh-
ter' come to mind. Ironically, they have learned by observing people who
think it's OK to promote a sales person, give them no formal training and
then just let them get on with it. The result is that they often struggle with
the basic requirements, for example, having to enforce discipline or new
working processes with people who were previously their colleagues and
peers.

It's not just sales. The same 'development principle' applies to financial
people, and all the rest. This is the way many companies find their leaders
– who often have no more qualifications other than success in their particular arena. It rarely works.

Despite there being numerous training courses, not enough companies
seem to see their value. Leadership, communication skills, assertiveness,
project management, an understanding of employment law and just basic
planning skills are not passed on to these previously successful people
who can find themselves running departments or even whole companies.
They may be making profits, but they are also making people miserable.
The long-suffering underlings pay the price, as the tantrums, moodiness
and fears of the shaky boss infect the workplace. And it's self-perpetuat-
ing: they will go on to promote people in the same way, so that in the end,
no one benefits, including the organisation. Marvellous!

Stress in the news

The Times May 16th 2005

Britain counts £100bn cost of stress in the workplace

STRESS at work is causing depression and anxiety in one in five Britons and costing the country £100 billion a year in lost output, the mental health charity MIND said yesterday. Mental health problems have replaced back pain as the main reason why people claim incapacity benefit and do not work. Not only are stress and anxiety responsible for 45 million lost working days a year but they reduce the effectiveness of many who do not take sickness leave, MIND said. The charity's report distinguishes between stress which can lead to a downward spiral of physical and mental ill health, and positive pressure at work, which can motivate.

Among the causes of workplace stress are poor working conditions, personality clashes and employer's failure to take stress seriously.

Early warning signs include insomnia, fatigue, muscle tension, palpitations, breathlessness without exertion and headaches.

Psychological warning signs included an inability to concentrate, sense of humour failure, high levels of anxiety, constant irritability or withdrawal from social contact.

If left untreated excessive stress could eventually lead to a suppression of the immune system. If severe it could lead to a range of medical, psychological or behavioural disorders.

Research by the Health and Safety Executive suggests that 20% of employees suffer from stress levels described as 'very' or 'extremely' stressful.

The TUC reported 58% of workers complained of stress because of their jobs.

Richard Brook, the chief executive of MIND, called for more openness about stress and mental health problems in the workplace. 'The Government should take a lead in tackling the stigma that is attached to mental ill health', he said.

The charity called for changes in working practices to give employees genuine control over their work and an appropriate degree of self management of workload. It said that roles should be clearly demarcated with defined responsibilities and expectations.

Warning signs

- Poor relationships, including low levels of trust, lack of supportiveness and adequate opportunities to explain problems to someone who will listen.

- Poor working conditions including long hours, shifts, travel, smells, poor lighting, noise, work overload and work underload.

- An unclear role, including poorly defined expectations, conflicting priorities, role conflict and responsibility for others.

- Personality including a tendency towards anxiety, or a disposition that is unsuited to the type of work. Extraverts for example may find a socially isolating job more stressful than introverts.

Chapter Three
The Nine Profiles

Help is here

When it comes to dealing with difficult bosses, there is no point in reinventing the wheel. Throughout history people have written about their experiences with dealing with bosses. You will find this theme in the Roman comedies, the Greek tragedies, Shakespeare, and every period of drama, including modern soaps and comedies. In other words, when it comes to coping with these characters, you are not alone, and never have been. Does it help to know this? You should feel reassured, because throughout recorded time, other people have had to deal with similar issues – whether it was building pyramids, or building computer networks. And you can learn from them. However, wherever possible, it is also a good idea to have someone close at hand you can trust – a partner or friend – with whom you can confide, discuss, and explore options.

If you have previously hidden work problems from a loved one, not wishing to burden or worry them with the feelings you are having about your job, you will need to be a little patient and explain things carefully. They will believe you have coped before, what are you complaining about now? They may initially be dismissive about your comments, but try to understand their reactions in the context of your previous communications. Tell them clearly about the situations you are experiencing and how you will appreciate their support to help you find a sustainable resolution, whatever that may be.

Talking always helps, but it is not a cure. Find someone who will listen to you, with whom you can bounce ideas around. Don't insist that they understand your particular situation, because, by definition, every personal experience is unique. Anyone who says "I know exactly how you must feel" is not going to be the right person; you need someone who will challenge your perceptions, and get you to think outside of your box. Your friend is there to help you move out of your blinkered view and get a broader perspective. They need to ask you questions of the 'what else' and 'what would happen if ...?' kind. As you begin exploring this unknown territory you will get ideas for how you could change, and incorporate the techniques described here.

One way into this often untalked about territory will be to understand the experiences of the people I have encountered in my career, and which are explored in the case studies. Even the mildest experiences discussed are still examples of poor management style. The worst bosses create complete misery in people, causing them to be ill to the point of needing medication, often ruining careers and family life, and making the innocent parties – children, partners and friends miserable too. The mildest can just cause a general cloud of unhappiness, which also unfortunately can mean the offending boss being able to perpetuate their reign for many years. Most of us have been in situations that lie somewhere in-between these two scenarios. However, the bottom line is: if it's making you unhappy, it matters. You have to consider improving the situation.

The Profiles

The profile names:

- *Friend Then Foe Then Friend Again*
- *Mr Long Hours*
- *Power Crazy Boss*
- *No Power Boss*
- *I Hired You, Now I Hate You*
- *Sales Manager*
- *Fear Merchant*
- *Small Business Owner*
- *Boss In Love*

Reading some of the following scenarios may increase your anger or unhappiness for a while as you recognise the frustrations of each situation. The behaviour of bosses can seem terrible and completely unacceptable – but remember that these people are generally inflicting this misery in ignorance. Honest. If you believe that, you are already shifting to a better position, to a position that will help you to change things

Chapter Four

Friend Then Foe
Then Friend Again

Quick check this boss:

- Moody
  - ◆ What will he be like today? This afternoon?
- Aggressive
  - ◆ Why didn't he just ask me? No need to shout!
- Inconsistent
  - ◆ Yesterday he said to do it the other way!
- Forgetful
  - ◆ That's not what we agreed!
- A loner
  - ◆ Why doesn't he sit with the team?
- Scruffy
  - ◆ Looks like he could take better care of himself

This boss links closely to:

- *Mr Long Hours*
- *I Hired You, Now I Hate You*

I think you will recognise this one straightaway. Our first case study comes from Stacey. Stacey was in her late twenties when she was headhunted by an American software company based in central London, to be part of a small sales team. The company had an HQ in the US and about 15 employees in the UK. Stacey told me about the company and how it was positioned. The business was described to her as having 'software solutions' which, whilst they were complex and 'cutting edge', were applications that had practically no competition in the market.

Stacey is a typical sales person. Highly motivated by success and praise, she had always performed best when in an environment where she received recognition for her skills. Coming from a young, energetic team who bounced ideas around, worked closely and with lots of support, the small intense 'start up' environment she was about to encounter would be a challenge …

Stacey's story

The role: sales and business development for a software company.

Stacey remembers how well it started. She had a very smooth interview process. The managing director, to whom she was to report, held three interviews, one of which was a very touchy-feely role-play session. "How enlightened," she thought!

In this story, we shall call the MD Peter. Stacey recalls how charming he was.

> "I remember he was very keen to tell me about how profitable the company was. He told me that there were great career opportunities as the company was expanding rapidly. Peter seemed relaxed and professional.

> "Looking back I probably should have asked more about Peter's background and the company's management team based in the US. He had given me pretty specific details on the financial state of the company. As my previous company had always been struggling with financial problems, it was just a relief to have the prospect of being with a suc-

cessful company. I was really excited about the prospect of having the opportunity of being with such a professional outfit and was flattered about being headhunted for the first time."

Reflecting on her experience, Stacey could see her first mistakes. Peter had made her feel very welcome, conducted a very thorough interview process, and communicated a very positive view of the company. It would have been difficult for either of them to have really faulted this part of the process – except that Stacey hadn't asked enough questions of her future new boss. Additionally, she didn't ask to speak to any members of the team she was to join, and worst of all, she was attracted by the financial position of the company, and used that as the main criteria for her decision to join. Cash flow had been a big problem at her previous company, so the appeal of the new company's financial security was a big part of her feeling good about the decision to join.

This is a good example of how, as in other relationships, we can react in a mercurial way to given traits, status, personality or any other stimulus. We are drawn to situations that appear to be the antithesis of former experiences. But in the world of job-hunting this is a mistake. Although it's tough, it's essential that you look at situations (vacant) in an objective state of mind. Of course you want to work for a successful company with a healthcare scheme, a subsidised canteen, and your own parking space. But what matters more are the people you are surrounded by and with whom you will interact on a daily basis. Those are the key factors that will most strongly influence your personal success and happiness.

Peter was charming, smiled freely and painted a wonderful picture. Stacey couldn't wait to start. The organisation was doing so well. She was just what they had been looking for. She would be a great addition to the team. When can she start?

On the surface everything seems well organised. Stacey is looking forward to working with her new boss, whom she can see is very keen and works hard. The job will be a challenge; there are deadlines and targets. As she passes through the office after her final interview and receiving the job offer, everyone in the modern quiet office seems very focused. What a great opportunity …

Stacey then told me how in the space of two to three weeks her fantastic new opportunity turned into her own personal hell.

The profile type in this story is the boss who seems to be unsure of how friendly to be. They don't really know how to manage people, and, as in many of our examples, will have had no training. One minute they are helpful and supportive, and the next they are aggressive and distant. Stacey's story is an excellent example of this particular profile, because, as you will soon find out, Peter exhibited amazing extremes of these behaviours. This profile is often the successful employee who is promoted as a 'reward', but not given the training and therefore the tools to complete their new role. Perhaps from this view we might start to see that the scenario goes beyond the responsibility of these two unhappy players, Stacey and Peter.

Stacey smiled broadly, as she continued her story (she says the smile is only possible because she has now left the job). Unfortunately, in this example, Stacey was not able to create a survival strategy, so the tactics for coping with this profile are supplied by another person who has managed to survive this all too common *Friend Then Foe Then Friend Again* boss. Sadly, Stacey did not have the benefit of this information.

> *"I will never forget the first time I became aware of the terrible flaw in Peter's management style. During the first couple of days we spent a lot of time together, he wanted to get me up to speed on the product as soon as possible. It was the steepest learning curve I had ever experienced. The pace was unrelenting and after a week I was exhausted; the trouble was, so was Peter. He was trying to train me but trying to do his own job as well.*

> *"I had joined on an understanding that (just like my previous roles) it would be normal to work from home a couple of days a week. Towards the end of the second week I approached Peter to ask if, as I had a lot of reading and research to do, he would mind if I spent the next two days studying at home. He turned suddenly and rounded on me; he was not the calm smiling man who had welcomed me to the 'team' less than a fortnight earlier. I was so shocked. He could have simply said that he would prefer me in the office but he became very angry and started shouting, 'I am not here to support you! You are*

producing nothing! You need to be out in front of customers! You need to get this stuff and get it quickly!' I was absolutely gobsmacked. He was furious. One question I had asked at interview was 'how long is the typical sales cycle and he had answered, 'six to nine months', so to be 'producing' anything one fortnight into the job was preposterous. I didn't understand what had changed; why was he suddenly so angry? He had gone from charm personified, all smiles and high fives, to a snarling, vicious, angry little boy. He reminded me of my sister's two-year-old child. He berated me for my selfishness and lack of commitment; he was sulky and cross. I was so upset I apologised and said I would come to the office and that it was no problem. I just didn't know how to react and was shocked at the strength of his reaction. I was too scared to remind him about our agreement about home working. I left the office that night feeling completely unsure of myself and not looking forward to going back the next day. I kept going back over the events of the previous ten days and couldn't understand why he seemed to be like a different person.

"*I had been attentive and engaged while Peter went through the product training and had not given him a single reason to doubt my commitment. I was genuinely excited about the role as I would be able to travel throughout Europe and would be opening doors at a very high level in top companies; I had made a career out of being enthusiastic and positive, what had I done wrong?*

"*The next day added to my confusion. Peter apologised for being angry and was smiling again. He said that what had happened was 'tension' and it was his style to be 'emotional'. I was so relieved, what was I worried about? Obviously there was nothing to be concerned about. It was just me – I was tired and anxious, and I wanted to do a good job. I didn't want them to have any regrets about hiring me.*

"*But it became a vicious circle. I would ask for something, I would ask for some information, I would ask for a reminder on a product detail, and he would react – and it was almost always the same. He made such a fuss over every answer, he made me feel really stupid, but I knew they were reasonable questions – at least at first I did. But the more annoyed he was at my questions, the more anxious and 'stupid'*

I became. I would repeat questions, forget answers and I slowly found my confidence being eroded away. I was so anxious and worried about every word I said, thinking it was going to be shot down as 'wrong', I was getting worse and worse. I felt tired all the time and started to feel ill. His constant correcting of my answers and then his comments about wondering about having made a mistake at my 'calibre' really got to me. I felt so unhappy; I felt it was not tenable for me to stay.

"Some people would have been stronger, I know, but that's how it affected me. In sales you are only regarded as successful when you start bringing in deals. I was under so much pressure, it prevented me from learning effectively and I was feeling my confidence slipping. It just wasn't the way to manage me. Generally sales people want encouragement, a bit of 'rah-rah' to get them going and some enthusiastic support. This boss was just watching for every chance to criticise and trying to find my cracks and weaknesses. In the end he was the one creating them."

So after only a few weeks, Stacey found herself under enormous pressure from a highly-stressed boss, who was demanding completely unreasonable things, constantly criticising her, and being very aggressive and sarcastic. She would not know where she stood from one day to the next. The sessions with Peter where he expressed his frustration with her performance were interspersed with times, sometimes even a few hours at a time, of him being very friendly, passive and patient. But sometimes he would be almost schizophrenic in his behaviour, turning into a snarling, whining, angry and aggressive child at the drop of a hat, not normally prompted by anything more than a simple question or a simple statement. Stacey was a professional sales person who had asked about the typical sales cycle, understood the sector if not the detail of the product, and was punctual, motivated and loyal. Within weeks she had become demotivated, anxious, tired and felt her confidence ebbing away.

Stacey continues:

"I felt that the minute I spoke to him in a 'normal' way, tried to make a little joke or comment he would change. He would let you get so close and then turn. There was no science in it. Sometimes a comment that had been acceptable on other occasions would make him distant

and cool. It was absolutely terrible; I cannot tell you how unnerving this can be over time. It's like a sort of torture. You need to build relationships and trust with the people you work with, but I just couldn't work him out, or understand where I stood from one day to the next. I was not the only person who felt like this in the office. Many of the others had seen him get like it over the four years he had been there, had worked with him as a colleague before his promotion, and did not take his tantrums to heart like I did. They were used to him, they sometimes got mad and answered him back, but I felt I couldn't do this. I was the new sales girl, trying to prove my worth, and he was the boss. I couldn't imagine talking to him like some of them did. They all said he had got worse over time."

What was going on? Was her boss mad? He had paid a big fee for her and spent hours in a recruitment process. What would make him behave in this way? Had something changed?

Stacey left the company after seven months. She did secure a couple of deals, but in her words the experience was like torture. She even walked away from a sizable commission cheque; the misery she was being forced to endure made her feel it was just not worth it. Stacey took a couple of weeks to look at the market and secured a new sales role with a much larger company.

"Where I had joined Peter's company because I was going to be the big fish in a small pond, with my new role I actively searched for a much larger company where I would not come under so much focus. I can remember studying the sales manager who interviewed me. I remember I asked him if he had had any training. He had been a little surprised and told me he had not but that 20 years in the role had given him enormous experience. I can remember I then asked if I could speak to one of his team alone. Again he was surprised but allowed it. I did not tell him about my previous experience, but that was what it had taught me. This company had a structured training programme that gave you time and resources to learn about the product. Looking back, there are other questions I could have asked, but even just asking these two things made me more secure about accepting the job. I knew from the talk I had with the team before I joined that he was a

reasonable, mature person, and that I could expect to be successful. It was like a breath of fresh air to work for my new boss, and I wished I hadn't stayed so long with the other company – it nearly destroyed me."

Stacey made the choice to leave, so we cannot learn from her what alternative strategies she could have employed. Maybe the lesson here anyway is: You don't have to put up with bad bosses. There are enough companies out there looking for good people and treating them well – so join one of those.

Quick note on the interview process

Remember that an interview is a two-way process, so interview your new boss! As a recruitment consultant, I can remember telling people to learn as much as they could about the company they were looking to join. Now I would say that an essential part of this is to check out the background of the boss.

What could Stacey have done if she had decided she wanted to see it through and stay? How do you deal with such a difficult situation? People's personalities dictate to a great degree what actions they are able to take. Telling someone in Stacey's position to just 'ignore him and get on with it', as some of her colleagues had suggested, was not going to work. She had to have, like many of us, a reasonable, harmonious work environment where she felt valued, and encouraged.

Mad Peter?

Now we will look at why Peter may have behaved in that way. His promotion path explains some of his behaviour. Managers who have been promoted from 'the team' often struggle with their credibility with their old colleagues. Even if the team accepts that he was certainly the man for the job, he cannot be sure of the new boundaries he has to maintain in terms of authority and discipline and of how friendly or sociable he can be. Racked with insecurity, he worries if his old team mates are taking advantage of their relationship to pull the wool over his eyes. Do they really respect and accept his authority? Because he was once part of the team, what does that count for now? Does that affect what he can allow them to 'get away' with? Peter suddenly feels isolated and starts doubting some of his decisions.

One day he comes into the office seeking positive interaction with the team he has worked with for years, and asks them to join him for a beer after work. He is generally affable and calm. But as the day progresses, one colleague calls in sick, another asks to leave early for the dentist while another has forgotten to make a phone call. All of a sudden, these petty instances combine to make him feel that he is a soft touch, that he is being taken advantage of. Full of latent fears and feeling isolated, he overreacts and spins into a cycle of unreasonable retribution. Everything is wrong, no one appreciates his difficult position, and warning letters are threatened, left, right and centre!

This is an extreme example; the staff issues are completely minor and his reaction is over the top. Does this model fit a boss you know? Anyone struggling with their own insecurities is difficult to get close to, hard to please. They see any close relationship as potentially threatening, and have to constantly reassert themselves as the boss, even if what they really want – as all human beings do – is to be included, and to be liked. The strain of being isolated – promoted by his managers and then left high and dry with not even a day of management training – means that Peter has become tired and irritable. He is desperate to succeed and prove to his bosses that they have made the right decision. He must not fail. But he is behaving in a way that will lose him the main thing he needs – his team and their support. Now he cannot judge a reasonable request from his staff without wondering if it's being asked as a favour.

This profile is just as likely to turn up on a construction site, a factory or a shop floor, as an office. Peter is himself a victim of a mad boss. Although you may understand the situation, what you really need to know is how to intervene to change things, for your own sake, to maintain your sanity on a day-to-day basis.

The isolation, the fear of failure, the lack of trust are the key elements behind his behaviour. Combined with tiredness and the feeling of not being respected, this creates the dual personality of the *Friend Then Foe Then Friend Again* boss profile.

This mad boss has his focus so targeted on delivering for his bosses, that he does not recognise the value of learning about how to manage or lead a team.

Peter could have avoided all this. After about a year as a manager he should have left and joined another company as a manager. The new company/team would only ever have seen him as a manager and would behave accordingly – a major part of his baggage would have been shed, and no old team members would be there to haunt him.

We will explore the practical ways to manage this type of environment. Always remember that even though your boss seems mad, he may not be bad. These strategies, which will save your sanity, are not at the expense of his. In all these examples, if you are able to step back and understand why your boss is having difficulty, you are halfway there …

The strategy for dealing with Peter

The first step for dealing with this profile is to learn how to interview prospective employers effectively. Even though you recognise the type, don't necessarily let this kind of boss put you off a job. If the company and the role fit, and match the salary you are after, this boss profile will become the perfect backdrop against which you will shine. When you understand not only his fears and drivers but also your own value and power, and the timing of when to use those powers, you will be able to deal confidently with them. You have so much ammunition, and I will show you how to use it. You don't have to suffer the misery of the *Friend Then Foe Then Friend Again* boss.

Realising your value goes a long way to altering your perspective on your job and will help to relieve immediately some of the stress you may be feeling.

Let's suppose you have joined a company like Peter's and found yourself in a miserable existence.

In many cases the reason for the misery is that the employee (or individual in any area of life) feels they have lost control, or cannot manage the situation in which they find themselves. They are in a place where they are on a hiding to nothing. Although they are fulfilling their brief, they are not actually having the effect they want. As Stacey remembers,

> "Whatever I did, it seemed to be wrong. I lost track of how I could answer him, of how I could succeed in the job."

So how do you get back control and stop the misery? Can you get the boss to understand the effect they are having on you? Can you help the boss be a better boss? Can you help this boss at all?

The first thing you can do is so simple. Do it tomorrow and find out how it changes things. Now, I understand some people will imagine it will require all their confidence, but let me assure you that confidence builds from success, and from there grows organically. Once you start flexing your 'confidence muscles' you will feel the strength growing. Work them and you will be surprised how far they will carry you.

Getting control back, the strategy of changes

All you have to do is to behave in ways that you have not done before. Change your responses: react or don't react but just behave in the opposite way to what you used to do. Ask questions; be curious. Make physical changes (I'm not suggesting plastic surgery – read on), postural changes, voice changes. Restate reasonable but previously unsatisfied requests. Make sure the company is treating you correctly and in conformity with your contract.

Redraw the lines of what is acceptable and what is not, but within the 'rules' of the company itself. You don't have to do anything more than just start to slowly let it be known that (and we are assuming you are unhappy here) you are not going to accept poor treatment any longer. It can be a gentle, slow process, but do start it!

Becoming 'a different person' means that you will seem different to people, including your boss, and they will have to react to you differently.

The main thing is that as you make these changes, don't tell anyone: this must be part of your strategy. You want them guessing and looking to you. You will need to be strong willed if you are normally the sort of person who avoids conflict or is susceptible to pressure, or frequently find yourself bursting to tell or explain. Remember how much as a kid you would pester a friend who had 'a secret'?

That is the sensation you are trying to create. It will intrigue your boss. What are you up to? Because you appear to have some special power or knowledge they will very much want to know just what it is. This might seem petty, but I can assure you that, if you carry this through correctly, it will cause an immediate pivotal shift in the power base in your relationship with the boss. You don't want to upset him (but it will happen anyway!), but you can't have him taking you for granted. The good news is you can do this in steps that are manageable for your level of comfort.

For every change you make, your confidence will grow. And for every change, other people's perception of you alters accordingly. The true measure of confidence is to say nothing and wait to be asked – and then people will be listening. This is the essence of 'cool': do not justify, do not explain why.

Practical Changes

■ *Arrive on time.* If you always arrive late because the train you normally take means you cannot get to work on time get an earlier one, even if it means arriving very early. If traffic means you are normally late, get up earlier, leave half an hour earlier, and get to work early or at least on time. If your childcare arrangements mean you are struggling to make the required start, make changes.

■ *Change your appearance.* Get a new haircut or style, but (so long as anyone notices) don't launch into discussions about it. If you normally turn up for work dressed like you slept in your clothes get a sharp suit. Conversely if you normally dress like you are going to the races, dress down. Get casual; keep smart.

■ *Alter your behaviour patterns.* If you are the person in the workplace who normally diffuses situations with humour, stop. If you normally don't join in with the jokes, start telling them.

■ *Adjust your voice.* When you have to communicate a problem does your voice go three octaves higher? Stop whining. Control your voice. See the power you can get from just lowering your voice. The words "I really need you to explain that again" become loaded with power if spoken slowly and low – go on try it! Compare the impact with communicating the same content as a high-pitched defensive complaint.

■ *Move and stand differently.* (You may need to notice how you usually do these things, as they are often out of awareness.) Posture and movement tell other people a great deal about your status – whether you are higher or lower than them.[1] Adjust your posture. If you find yourself crossing your arms, unfold them; most people know a little about the power of body language and have heard how this conveys aggression or defensiveness. Change the way you make eye contact. If you are in the habit of avoiding eye-contact, then it is essential that you learn to look the boss in the eye.

When you start combining your new low, slow-spoken questions while keeping eye contact, you have started to get your control back. It's a good idea to practise on your friends first, and ask them for feedback on how you are coming across.

1. For further information on the practical aspects of this, see Keith Johnstone, 1999, *Impro for Storytellers*, pages 219–246.

Stacey had always been able to make eye contact, and as a sales person understood how to use body language, but even so, she had trouble saying what she really wanted to say and saying it in a way that got noticed.

"Looking back, I know I probably didn't manage to tell him just how difficult I was finding it. I just blamed myself, and really that was part of the problem of my confidence fading. He made me feel stupid. I needed to tell him he was not delivering the training I required, nor allowing me time to get things done."

Ask questions. If a new company procedure does not make sense or seems wrong – question it, don't accept it. You will not need to be aggressive, just ask. For example, let's suppose that Stacey had not been so keen, had refused to struggle to learn from her stressed irritable boss. She should never have been put under such pressure at this stage of her training and could have said, slow, low and calmly:

"You are so busy; you are not explaining things well enough. I need more time to understand."

"We could shorten my learning cycle if you could dedicate some time to teaching me."

If at the time you joined, your contract said you would receive certain tools or training, make sure you have had them all. Don't roll over and accept that the contract is generally treated with lip service. If you were promised a mobile phone for business but somehow you ended up using your own, then ask for what you should have. This is not being aggressive, but assertive!

You will discover the power of not behaving as people expect. Maintain first-class work, stick to the rules, and stop being an open book. Certainly your boss will start behaving differently, though he may not be able to say why. He will probably begin to feel some of the insecurity that he has put you through, not knowing how you will react, not being able to assume how his instructions will be handled, and realising that you are now questioning where perhaps before you were passively accepting.

- Say nothing. There is no need to justify or explain your behaviour, because that's how you create the 'secret'.

- Change how you speak to your boss – make the content assertive, not aggressive.

- Change as much of your behaviour as possible to create a new you – easy stuff, but powerful.

Next steps

Changing your behaviour is a first step – but there is more work to be done. Bosses with the classic *Friend Then Foe Then Friend Again* boss profile do have windows of time when they are extremely friendly and pleasant. This is the problem: you are never quite sure which way they will flip. So you need to use these windows to your advantage. The temptation is to be very friendly in return. It's such a relief to bathe in the sunshine of his friendliness. You are momentarily relaxed and laugh at the jokes. You believe you are getting to know him better …

In this situation, somewhere in the back of your fragile mind, you hope you are building a relationship with him, one that will stand you in good stead when you next need support, understanding, or merely the answer to a question. If you actually believe that he will look at you differently the next time you ask for assistance or advice, you are wrong – VERY WRONG!

Pandering to his need to feel liked and included does not demonstrate your changed behaviour. All it does is keep his game going. It is likely that he will deeply regret being friendly and, when the opportunity (reason) next arises, will be even more distant, aggressive and unhelpful – leaving you with that feeling that he must be schizophrenic. He is afraid that he has been too friendly and may have left himself open to being 'taken advantage of'. In this mindset he makes a U-turn, feeling he must remind you of his position as the boss! That is why he can one minute be treating you like his best mate and then suddenly become cool and unfriendly.

When he is in a friendly mode, a more effective strategy is to not be friendly in return. Instead, be a little distant and aloof, criticise him. This, of course, must be done very, very carefully. Remember that during these friendly windows he is fulfilling his need to feel liked and included, and you are in effect telling him (or at least behaving as if) you don't like him. Treat this as a gradual process, increasing the level every time you get the opportunity.

He's like a mother crocodile who, having just watched her eggs hatch, has her normal killer instinct suppressed long enough for her to carry the babies in her mouth to the safety of the river. Your boss in 'I need to feel included and liked' mode has his reactive, aggressive button switched to 'off'. He is feeling pretty 'self-congratulatory' at that moment, he has convinced himself that not only is he a great boss, but he can still be part of and liked by the team! This would be a difficult one to snap out of!

He will listen; information will be absorbed. Repeat the process. Don't fall into the trap of being too friendly again too quickly. If he wants you to like him, let him earn it.

It can be a very mild conversation to start. He won't even notice. "Peter, I was wondering about your decision to cancel the training last week? What came up?" He talks, you listen attentively. You are trying to find out what is motivating him, what kind of pressure he is under. You are pressuring him, slightly.

Build the questioning over time: gently asking him, reminding him carefully – not aggressively – about situations where he let you down or was possibly unreasonable. You may even be able to tell him you sometimes find it difficult to talk to him. It is essential to keep out of the 'hope he will like me' mode. Keep the questions going over time, building them till you could ask, "Why did they make you boss? Have you ever had any training?" and get a reasoned answer. Your end goal is to tell him that the way he is managing you is not as good as it could be, that it's not the best way to motivate you, and it's making you very unhappy.

When you are able to start articulating these sorts of ideas and concepts to your boss there is another level to which you may be able to progress. If he can learn through these coherent, friendly exchanges that you are a person he can talk to and trust, you may be able to start discussing the bigger issues faced by the company. He may start to share some of the problems he is facing with you in your new found 'advisor role', subjects such as the pressure he is under, and how well he is coping with the difficult challenges set by his bosses. Congratulations! If you have reached a level of communication which offers the opportunity for tackling these problems, and if you can maintain this level of relationship throughout the average working day, then you are having a real effect on the mad boss. By being part of a team that shares the boss's issues and is involved in trying to solve them, you should derive a great deal of satisfaction from your role.

You probably need to practise your new behaviour of not falling into friendly mode whenever it suits the boss. If you are serious about keeping your sanity, you must try it. Remember, that any change feels odd and unfamiliar at first. Therefore you need to do things until they become second nature. So give it a chance to succeed before changing your mind about following it through.

Vanity is a great tool. The more you give attention to someone, take an interest in their well-being, in their career, the more sought after your opinions become to that person. You are asking your boss things no one else asks. This too effects their mindset. Build on showing an interest in their life by asking these questions. Now is the time to start making suggestions ...

Come on – get creative!

Start to tell your boss stories. You are going to tell him about your experiences with your favourite ex-bosses. Storytelling is the way to get change, as long as you tell the right story. (It also helps to have had the right boss in the past upon which to draw from for the stories – but if you didn't – never mind. You just need to invent your perfect boss in your imagination.)

Describe to your boss how you would like them to speak to you, based on what worked for you in a previous role. How you like to be managed, encouraged and supported. If you are making up your perfect ex-boss traits, it may help to use the experiences of a friend or colleague who has worked for the real person. Build your own 'best practice' boss, even if it's made up from your imagination or other people's experiences, and then tell you boss about them. It's a way to plant good boss behaviour ideas into your mad boss's brain. Tell him the story …

> *"Do you know, Peter, one of the best bosses I ever worked for used to hold 'company picnics' once a month. We would send out for food and everyone would join in for lunch. It was a great opportunity to introduce new team members and was great for morale and communication, and it was all in our lunch hour."*

> *"I don't know about you, Peter, but one of the most successful bosses I worked for used to hold team amnesty meetings; you could say what you liked without fear. We used to really learn from the mistakes we'd made, and that meant that instead of covering things up and making the same mistake two weeks later, we improved processes enormously. The benefits to the company were amazing."*

You are not criticising him. If the poor devil has never had any training he may not have heard of any of these things before. And you don't need training either; just imagine the best work environment you can. It might be a good idea to make a note of the main points you give to your boss, as a reference – you don't want to look inconsistent. In fact one of the requirements for the success of this strategy is to be extremely consistent. At no point can you exhibit any of the vacillating mood traits of your boss. And remember, if the call should ever come, think how well prepared you will be for management …

There can be no definite timescale for the strategy outlined above. It will almost certainly be months, in which time you will have been enjoying planning your questions and creating your 'best practice' boss.

- Be consistent and persistent
- Keep your stories straight
- Don't behave like your boss; stay predictable, consistent, cool-headed
- Make sure you have choices – some other strategies that you can use

Move up a level

You have now started to get somewhere. It's not an overnight process; such changes take time. Enjoy changing yourself and watching those around change too. See how far you can go with the questioning. Push it!

Having one process is a good start. But there are other things you can do to ease your misery. This next strategy should be available to most people in largish organisations. You are going to build a network of contacts at his level or above. If at all possible, you will get to know your boss's boss!

This ploy of getting to know the boss's boss fascinates me on two levels. Firstly, you get to find out the extent to which they are aware of the behaviour defect in your boss; and secondly, you get a measure of their loyalty – or rather, their complete lack of loyalty in discussing him with you. So what is the purpose of developing this connection with the bosses boss? Well, it's unlikely that training courses will be on the agenda – these are the bosses of the mad boss.

Peter is like a stroppy, aggressive child. He is domineering. He believes that he can behave like this because he is the boss: "It's my world/department/section, and I'm in control!" You do as he says, who is there outside this little empire who will believe or support you? He is certainly behaving as if his approach is secret, he doesn't seem to worry about anyone finding out.

He has insecurities and you are going to play on them – but this is not to be approached with a cruel attitude. So many of the *Friend Then Foe Then*

Friend Again bosses are simply victims themselves of a misplaced 'reward' of management.

Use whatever pretext you can to get on friendly terms with your boss's boss. If there is no valid work reason, find another. Perhaps he likes pigeon-racing or stamp-collecting; whatever it is, use it to make contact and to communicate with him. You might have the opportunity of being introduced through a company social event. Whatever it is, just do it. However, once you have established the connection with Peter's boss, never criticise Peter in front of him. Remember that Peter does not have a mentor or boss who is helping to improve him; you may be the only person truly able to help this abandoned individual.

Here is a sample conversation that you could have with Peter. Peter's boss is called Gerald.

> Stacey:
> "*Hey Peter, I am still having problems getting the correct invoices out to the customers in the North.*"

> Peter:
> "*Well just sort it out! You know we can't survive if the invoices aren't sent! Why can't you just sort it?*"

> Stacey:
> "*Well, we were supposed to have had training on the accounts system but you cancelled it. I don't know how to put it together.*"

> Peter:
> "*God! Do I have to do everything around here.*"

> Stacey:
> "*I know. I was speaking to Gerald the other day; I wonder if he finds they have these training issues in the manufacturing division?*"

Bingo! He now knows you speak to Gerald. Gerald and you may only have spoken about stamp-collecting but he doesn't know that. If Peter speaks to Gerald, he will confirm he knows who you are. He will wonder, "What else is Stacey discussing with Gerald?" It is highly probable that Peter is beginning to feel insecure, and perhaps has an inkling that, for all he knows, his behaviour is known to Gerald. Maybe the behaviour is not acceptable to Gerald? Peter is wondering: "Perhaps Gerald thinks I can't cope?" "Does Gerald know I cancelled the training?" You need Peter to accept that his behaviour is not 'secret', that it is visible to other people in the company whom he may prefer not to know. Peter knows that some of his behaviour in the privacy of small meetings is 'questionable' – his shouting, criticising, being sarcastic – because he would not do those things in front of Gerald. Again, this makes him think twice.

Try this strategy. It is not a 'one size fits all' scenario but a somewhat simplified view. Remember that you have to start somewhere if you are to realise your own sphere of influence and not look or feel like a stand-alone victim. Do it, and feel the power!

Spread the word

Another way to check Peter's mad comments and statements is to make them 'public'. If he has made outrageous comments to you and your colleagues in a meeting (when he is playing The Boss in His World), refer to these comments when other bosses, managers or even visitors are around.

Peter was known for slamming his hand on the desk and telling people "you will never be successful at this company unless you are prepared to work through the whole weekend!" or "the only excuse for being late is if you are dead!" Now clearly these are stupid, crass and ignorant statements. So let's tell everyone! But for maximum impact do it in front of him. Turn to your colleague in a meeting with the various audiences as indicated above, and say, "Don't forget, Peter said we will never be successful unless …" and so on. This has to be done is a totally dead-pan style. There must not be a hint of irony. You are simply repeating something Peter said, so it must be right, mustn't it?

Will Peter reflect more carefully on his comments to you once he discovers that there is the possibility that you will share these (ridiculous) statements with this wider audience? Oh yes, I think he will. How can these stupid statements be viewed as anything other than damaging to his image? Peter will in future take more care in the way he communicates his philosophy.

There is another outcome to this particular part of the strategy. If you are very good it is possible, in showcasing these terrible comments in the right, ridiculous light, to make it a funny event. If Peter could have laughed at himself for making these comments, could he have reflected on them, and seen for himself what he was really doing? However, this advice will have to be taken on a 'per boss' basis. If you know your boss has no sense of humour and is unlikely to be able to see any humour in this situation, do not risk using it.

Even though I have seen some ferocious, mad bosses reduced (or is that elevated?) to laughter when confronted by mimicry of their style, you must judge your own boss's likely reaction. This is more often something that only their peers can pull off.

Making these changes will already be giving you more of a feeling of power. You are beginning to take more control. The questions and suggestions put forward during the windows of friendliness will start to build a true relationship. You have modified some of your behaviours, you have manoeuvred to get to know his bosses and peers, so his behaviour (so far as he is concerned) is in the public domain, it's out. What else is left?

Resistance is … missing

Do you know how irritating it can be when people won't play your game, won't be baited into an argument, and constantly agree with you? "You're absolutely right." This actually puts them in a position where it's hard to follow on, hard to maintain any anger because they are initially surprised (agreement is unusual in our culture) and they are geared up for a fight. They now have all that adrenaline pumping away for nothing. You could think of this as the martial arts approach – simply let the verbal blows they issue bypass you without impact or pain. "I agree" will instantly deflate the inflated boss.

You will know that my advice will follow previous patterns. You don't actually have to agree with what they are saying, and may even go off and complete the task in question entirely in the way you decide, but for that moment, watching the wind leaving their sails is very satisfying and naturally puts the control firmly in your hands again. People cannot push where there is no resistance.

The technology solution

The next time you are due to have a meeting or training, tell him that you intend to record it. Recording devices are readily available. Get to know all your recording options. For example you can use the recording facility on your mobile phone to great effect. I realise that in the office or meeting environment it won't always be possible to whip out a recording instrument, but many of us have to communicate through mobile phones. Have you ever used the recording option on yours? When talking, if you think that the conversation is heading towards a crucial statement that needs recording just press the options button – the one showing while you are talking – and press the record option. Most will do a minute or two and it will be stored on the phone, date and time stamped! If the recording facility runs out, cut the call (blaming 'poor signal') and then call him back and record again.

Your reasoning for recording the meeting is that because there is so much to remember (he has as good as told you that you are stupid) you really want to understand, and you know that the repetition of your questions irritates him. So this way you can play back the meeting and hear the points/training/instructions at your leisure. It is a perfectly reasonable request. It shows initiative and demonstrates how keen you are to learn and improve(!)

The amazing result is that he is almost bound to agree. Your request is unassailably fair; you are showing your intelligence in wanting to get the most from the meeting. But, of course, we all know what else it's saying. "You, Mr Boss, have to do a good job. You cannot swear or get aggressive; you must be clear and professional and not resort to tantrums." More power! (And you get to learn, because you can go over the content of the meeting again and really understand the information it delivered. That's what I call a win-win.)

How often does the stressed irritable *Friend Then Foe Then Friend Again* boss say things that they later deny? I have experience of bosses saying one thing to me and then saying they didn't, or that I misunderstood. You are unlikely to ever need these recordings in a court of law but they can be incredibly powerful if used appropriately.

A word of warning: do not use any 'incriminating' recording in anger. Your power comes from choosing your moment, and you will choose the opening of one of the 'friendly boss' windows. Be a little smug. For weeks he may have taunted you for failing to remember something he told you, you will have taken a load of grief, but wait.

Wait for him to be in his friendly mood again, and then, preferably when he is again teasing you or telling a colleague about your mistake, at that moment, look concerned. Get out the phone and say, "I wonder if that's right … Let's just check." Remind him of the incident and, yes, make it all a good-natured big joke. Smile all the way, and play the recording back to him. Keep laughing: "amazing modern technology, isn't it?" It will be a long time before you will have to record anything again.

If you have email communication at work, use it to protect yourself: set up a folder to store all the emails you feel might be useful in future. Call this file something innocuous such as 'Drafts2'. Regularly send copies through to a private email address, or back them up regularly onto a memory-stick, so that you have a back-up copy available.

Practical and immediate

The strategies we have discussed may take some time to come to fruition. Some will work better for you than others, and some may not be options. I hope that at least they give you some ideas of your own.

Here is something you can do tomorrow, which carries minimal risk with the *Friend Then Foe Then Friend Again* boss. Talk more to your colleagues about your experiences, and how you feel. They may be in the position of knowing the boss before he was promoted. What was he like when he was at their level? Why was he promoted? Some quality must have high-lighted him as a suitable candidate (be prepared for possible expressions of professional jealousy). What were his good points? He was rewarded for his success, and you could learn a great deal from that. Perhaps there is something you have ignored or are missing out on? It's a great opportunity to learn from his experience.

Stacey joined a company at full stretch. If she could have spent more time talking to Peter's old team, she may have been able to have put things into perspective. The stories they can tell can take some of the sting out of what you are experiencing. They will tell you about the mistakes the boss made, how long it took him to learn and the clients or suppliers he annoyed – it's all good stuff, and all helps to put things into perspective.

Stacey's colleagues were all under so much pressure that it was difficult to find time to talk. This last option was not available to her. But this was also a sign of the unhealthy management of her office, which a good interview process may have revealed.

Finally

Don't let a boss like Peter let you lose faith in yourself. Remember your successes, where people liked you, where you enjoyed working. Remember what your friends think of you and your family. There is and always should be more to life than just work, but as we spend so much time doing it, we deserve to be happy in that environment.

Remind yourself that you can always learn from whatever situation you find yourself in. You can probably learn even more from people who are really bad than from those that are really good. If you ever find yourself in a manager/boss situation, you will remember all the things that you reacted badly to with your useless bosses and what motivated and inspired you.

It is through human contact that you will find a greater degree of happiness. Your success with these strategies will help you grow new relationships, both with your boss and with your colleagues.

The decision is with you, but there is one final idea I would suggest. If you are feeling dreadfully low, then take action by putting your head 'over the parapet'. Go and find another job, get to interview stage. Even if you are not planning to leave, you are in some way perturbing the universe, and something will change. This is such a great ego boost, and you will go back to work feeling full of that powerful elixir – confidence – because you are acting proactively at last! You may not have to hand in your notice because you feel capable of putting a strategy in place that will change your daily work experience. By going through this process you will have realised that you do have choices, and for every human being, including your boss, finding yourself in a situation where you believe you don't have any choices is the most depressing of all.

Managing a *Friend Then Foe Then Friend Again* boss

Summary:

- Make changes in your behaviour to keep him guessing
  - ◆ Stop trying to please him
- Use the moments when he is friendly to tell him how you feel
- Get to know his boss!
- Take him 'public'
  - ◆ Quote – and attribute – his dumb comments
- Use technology
  - ◆ Record those meetings!
- Talk to colleagues
- Check out your options
  - ◆ Remember your past successes

Chapter Five
Mr Long Hours

Quick check this boss:

- Depressing
  - ◆ He has squeezed all joy out of the place
- Nags you – but you know what you're doing
- Closed
  - ◆ Refuses or slow to try new ideas, processes or technology
- Doesn't like to delegate
  - ◆ Would it look like he couldn't cope?!
- Thinks long hours represent:
  - ◆ Loyalty
  - ◆ Dedication
  - ◆ 'Good work'

This boss links closely to:

- *Friend Then Foe Then Friend Again*
- *Power Crazy*
- *Fear Merchant*

OK, let's get this straight from the start. If your boss gets in really early in the morning and leaves very late at night, in relation to the rest of the company, then don't entertain any doubts – he is struggling! There is no way he can be doing a great job. Long hours at the workplace are an attempt to cover weakness and lack of ability. Your boss is not doing well; he comes across as a very anxious individual who is trying to keep a hold on his role.

On the other hand, his bosses are probably rubbing their hands in glee. They have found this guy who will work all God's hours, and think they are 'winning'. But they are wrong!

When a boss works very long hours his health will suffer: he will get tired, he will be ill, and he will make mistakes. The more mistakes he makes, the more moody, irritable and frustrated he becomes. And this is never the right man to run the organisation. There is a kind of warped logic which promotes these guys to boss status because of their long hours, based on the myth that working long hours means dedication, and that they are effective. Instead, long hours actually mean inefficiency and an inability to get the work done. Anyone exhibiting these symptoms is going to be stressed, unable to cope with the pressure and may soon become very sick.

So could this boss work shorter hours? Probably not. Because at the heart of this profile is this problem: "I work long hours and this has brought me this level of 'success'. If I were to work shorter hours and still attain success, that would make a mockery of my life and the way I have spent my time!" Along with this goes the belief that life is a struggle, and that success only comes with a great deal of effort. However, this is the effort that comes from working harder, not smarter.

Any boss like this becomes a bottleneck. They hold up the work because they are not efficient at processing it. A tired person makes decisions that are emotional and wrong, and this affects the overall health of the company, and leads to many kinds of suffering. I would definitely not advise employing this type of individual.

Working for such a boss is going to be a great challenge. *Mr Long Hours* will berate you for you lack of dedication, and do it loudly! The bottom line is that this is his way of trying to make you look bad and himself look like a dedicated hard worker. You, on the other hand, are probably coping well enough with your job, managing your time effectively and have a life outside of work. And that means you are motivated to do your work *within* the hours.

The boss may feel he has no choice but to make these pathetic noises. He may feel he has no one he can turn to explain his frustrations, or to help him to do his work better; he may just be poor at delegating. His bosses may not even realise he is struggling; he may constantly cover it up in front of his management.

Despite widespread reports of the 21st century workforce being well-placed to experience shorter working hours, this is not the reality[2]. In this world of targets, results, shareholders and time famine, every company is under great pressure and squeezes their pressured bosses to produce more and more out of less. This pressure, added to the lack of managerial training, means it is increasingly likely you will come across this scenario at some stage in your career.

It is essential to get the measure of the Long Hours type of boss, otherwise they will make your life a misery. When this boss interviews you, look out for warning signs such as bitten-down nails and a haggard-looking appearance. The conversation may flit between subjects quickly and in a disconnected way.

If you accept the job, and fail to take action to do anything about this boss, over time they will grind you down. They will constantly be nagging you about your time-keeping, being picky about your work, asking if you realise how lucky you are to have your job. All these are projections of his own insecurity. In his irritation he will repeatedly remind you of what he expects of you, because he imagines everyone is trying to short-change him on time. Should you succumb to his constant badgering, you may find yourself in the dangerous position of actually spending longer and longer hours in your workplace, hoping this will pacify his complaining. However, even if you think you are delivering what he wants, you can never meet his demands because the targets will always be shifting. Not only will this have a detrimental effect on your work, it will also affect your life outside of work, and contribute to damaging or even destroying it.

Before we look at the case study of Marcus, here are some thoughts about dealing with this type of boss. Many of the stresses we feel in this type of environment occur because we get too close to the situation. We may start

---

2. *Working Long Hours: a Review of the Evidence:* Volume 1 – Main Report, Kodz J, Davis S, Lain D, Strebler M, Rick J, Bates P, Cummings J, Meager N. DTI Employment Relations Research Series ERRS16, 2003.

to experience the tiredness that the boss is feeling, and like them, make incorrect, emotional decisions. In order to assess the issues as a whole and see what is really happening, you need to step back and take in the whole picture. Then you can see better what is pulling the levers and strings in your world, and find which ones to pull to your advantage.

Typically *Mr Long Hours* positions himself as a 'company man', hoping this will cover his weaknesses, and protect his activities from scrutiny. He aligns himself closely with all the ingrained (and sometimes completely wrong) company culture. Having totally absorbed this culture, he then 'talks the talk', referring to process and rules, going 'up the line', avoiding decisions, and displaying little or no creativity. He generally crushes any innovation that comes from his employees/team. Part of his profile means he will discard anything that may show himself as lacking in ideas – unless he can quickly rebrand them as his own. He is isolated. He is out of his depth and has no one coaching him.

Other traits of this boss may include a determination to keep excessive records of obsolete materials and believe this is good practice, but not know why. He expects respect but has no idea how to earn it – except through his Long Hours act. He is a boss for whom the right company mission statement might read:

> 'Remember working with [Company Name] is not a job, it's a lifestyle choice.'

Sadly, he would not realise the irony …

If you have ever worked for such a company, you probably pondered the origins of such strange bosses in this modern age. It's like discovering a strange missing link to a Dickensian world, a man (it would have to be a man) unmistakable by his tired, red-rimmed, puffy eyes and generally dishevelled appearance. You imagine him hunched on a stool in the corner of a dark candle-lit office, surrounded by dusty volumes, poring over obscure pages, hoping to avoid real human contact, and seeming to relish the suffering.

Whatever the mission statement he will know it off by heart. He will believe that an acceptable route to promotion is to wait for dead men's shoes. All in all, although variations exist, the classic form of the *Mr Long Hours* boss will make for an extremely unpleasant workplace.

In other words, you are up against a narrow-visioned boss who is unwilling to take responsibility for his own decisions. So what kind of future does he have? And how can you intervene to brighten your future prospects?

This is one of the boss profiles which creates a thick, tough glass ceiling for themselves. In latter years, as they wake up to their mistake and find themselves beating against the unbreakable glaze, drowning in the rising waters of efficiency and progress, they choke, and seeing the relative ease with which the people around them permeate through to success they wonder how they can have been rewarded in this way for their many Long Hours …!

So as long as you don't turn you into a long hours worker, you'll find that this boss will not be standing in the way of your career progress. In the meantime, he could still make your life a complete misery, so, to ensure that you do not end up in his position, you need to learn how to cope on a day-to-day basis.

Marcus's story

Marcus is in his mid-twenties. He joined a manufacturing company specialising in plumbing accessories, and worked in a large administration department of approximately 20 souls. The MD, George, was in charge of the business. The directors (the boss's bosses) were based in head office, about twenty miles away, which was the corporate base for the entire organisation which constituted a conglomeration of building material manufacturers.

Marcus had always worked hard, so when at the interview George told him it was sometimes necessary to put in 'a few extra hours', he had not taken too much notice. Marcus explained his story. Wearing an immaculate dark navy suit, he looked every inch the successful young executive:

> *"I just thought to myself, well, it's the modern workplace isn't it? I had never minded putting in some extra time, I always thought it was*

good for your career, can really get you noticed. George, yeah, well he did look a bit tired, but you have no idea do you? I just thought he seemed like a pretty decent old fella and I really wanted the job. It was a much bigger role than my previous job and I wanted the exposure to the corporation that owned the company."

Marcus had had the benefit of a degree in business administration and welcomed fresh approaches to situations. He was looking forward to using some of his education in improving business processes. He liked the fact that the company was well placed to benefit from some new thinking. It was an old, established organisation with a sizeable workforce, covering all aspects of manufacturing, distribution, sales, marketing, accounts and so on. A great opportunity, he thought.

After an unremarkable interview with George, the managing director, Marcus was offered the job. He was really pleased with himself! Although George was only about 42, he looked older. However, his appearance was not in accordance with what one might expect of a senior manager. His grey schoolboy socks stood out light against a dark, old crumpled suit. His silk tie was stained; his shoes were good quality but scuffed and dirty. Maybe this was what to expect with the type of company. During the interview George had once or twice referred to 'keeping head office happy', but any indication of his management failing (or trait) was hidden.

Marcus began his story,

"I can remember thinking, 'Hey, it might not be Microsoft, but here I can have an impact and see a company grow through making things more efficient, putting in employee incentive plans, better software systems, stock management' – all that good stuff I had learned about. It was going to be my first full blown operations manager role.

"I had a contract, of course, and when I started I had a girlfriend. I was also a regular player with the local rugby team, and I didn't want to give either of them up! So the stated hours of 9am to 5.30pm for my working day were notable in their blandness. I was where I wanted to be and had no idea that the 'old fella' who had been pleased to hire me was now going to show his true colours. It began on day one. I can remember being shown some of the rather antiquated computer

systems that managed things like the raw materials, procurement for manufacturing, stock control and the sales order process. At about half past five, being a first day, I felt exhausted and started clearing up my desk – getting ready to leave. I can remember looking around my office at the four or five guys who I shared with, it was odd. None of them moved, none looked like they were going home. I asked one guy what time they finished, and he shuffled uncomfortably in his seat, failed to make eye contact and said most people worked 'a bit late'. I was just too tired to stay and thought they certainly couldn't expect me to stay late on my very first day, surely?

"So, with a few uncomfortable coughs from my new colleagues, I gathered my things together and left the office."

Marcus's story is an example of a success story. We are going to show how a strategy implemented from a very early stage can bring a dramatic change. Even if you are already in this loop, the strategies are still relevant and will help you change your environment. As in the previous chapter, you will have to tweak some the ideas to make them work successfully in your own work context.

The next day and for the rest of the week Marcus resolutely stuck to his formal leaving time. He could see what was happening and luckily decided on a route of strategies which would enable him to resist the (up till now) silent demand that he stay longer.

Marcus, being a confident young man with an education that had prepared him for the business world, could see straight away that George was struggling with his role. It was obvious that George was maintaining control simply by using the Long Hours routine. Marcus had not experienced this situation exactly before, but all his business teachings reinforced the belief that anyone who worked like George was not up to the job. With his teachers' voices ringing in his ears, he found he did have the confidence to stick to what he had been taught, but he knew he would have to work out how to manage his new boss, and still make the impact in the office that would fit his promotion and career aspirations.

Marcus continues:

> *"It was predictable really. After the first week I was summoned to George's office and I was fairly sure I knew what was coming. George was extremely agitated. I felt very uncomfortable in his office, and felt like getting up and just walking out. He started asking why I was so lacking in commitment to the company and why did I feel I didn't need to work as hard as the rest of the team. Wasn't I serious about my career with the company? Did I realise how lucky I was? Etc, etc. I was expecting some fallout for my actions, reasonable as they were, but I was not ready for how angry and defensive the boss was. He was furious that I had flaunted the company culture. Despite the answers I had practised in my head, I found myself apologising. I said I would try harder, but in my heart I knew I wouldn't. I just wanted to get out of his office, away from his nagging, so I said anything to make him happy. But I knew deep down I would just stick to my guns more, not less. As soon as I got out of his office I felt relieved but wished I had behaved differently, but I did begin to sort out in my head how I was going to tackle the situation."*

Marcus did not manage to do anything constructive in this first uncomfortable meeting with George, but he did do something that you can use with many boss scenarios: buy yourself some time. This is often necessary when you are caught unawares by an extreme reaction or a dubious or unreasonable request. Marcus made all the right noises at the meeting to diffuse the situation with George; he now needed to go away and think about his strategy.

Taking a sickie

An extreme version of buying time is 'taking a sickie'. This I absolutely heartily recommend. Some bosses or managers may think this totally irresponsible advice ... It is not. If it's a choice between taking some time out to get some distance and perspective, to think about how you are going to manage your working life and move forward, or getting increasingly anxious, depressed or ill, then taking a sickie is without doubt the best option!

However, do not abuse this tactic or you could make the situation much worse. If you have a good record with regard to sick days, then when you have a crisis, or encounter a run of poor management, decide to act positively and take the day off!

I really must emphasise that if your boss causes you so much distress that you cannot think, are in fear, or need time to work out a problem or difficult situation, it is much better for your mental health to get some distance. Take that day to calm down, relax, think things through, so that you can return refreshed and with a clear strategy in mind.

The worst thing you can do is keep pushing yourself, feel guilty, increase the stress, and then become really ill. That will not only affect you but also your personal life and long-term plans. When people are sick or just low they do not make good decisions and are far more likely to lose control at work, make bad mistakes, or even, under very bad conditions, just walk out. Try not to let that happen.

Use your away-day profitably. Once the anger or guilt have subsided, get down to business – which is to return to work in a state of mind ready to deal positively with the issues facing you.

Some enlightened American companies (I have not heard of this happening in any British company) actually allow their employees what they call 'duvet days'. (You might think of these as sanctioned sickies.) It is an acceptance or recognition by management that employees sometimes just need to take time out to collect themselves, do something different, and refresh themselves before returning to work. Employees do not have to explain the reason for their absence; they just let the company know that they are taking a duvet day. Their contracts allow for one or two of these days per year. In an ideal world no one would be sick, stressed, over tired, and so on, and need this facility; but in a less-than-perfect world of work this solution recognises that by giving people this option the overall work environment will benefit. OK, it's enlightened self-interest, but it can be a life-saver for the employees.

Strategies for dealing with George

Marcus has already suggested one strategy for coping with the Long Hours boss. Sticking to the contract, firmly and politely, applies not just in this scenario, but across most types of boss profile. By ignoring the debilitating culture supported by *Mr Long Hours*, he will start to feel very uncomfortable indeed, because you are raising the thought that 'if it's possible for other people in this office/shop/factory to do their work within normal working hours, then why can't I?'

You really do need to make *Mr Long Hours* feel uncomfortable around you, so you are going to behave in ways that he may not have experienced before.

With the exceptions I am going to describe below, you will stick to your guns on the contracted hours and be extremely, unassailably pleasant about it. You will be training him, in the same way that you modify the behaviour of a naughty dog, the toddler with tantrums, or the moody teenager. You praise what's positive, and just ignore the bad, irritable or generally mediocre behaviour.

This could be challenging to do at first, especially if you are in an established position, as your boss may think you are taking the mickey (and in a way you are). But you must stick to it.

Pretend not to hear particularly nasty comments, or for example, if you are asked to perform a task that does not fit the strategy requirements you have decided upon (worked out on your duvet day/sickie). You vow to yourself that:

- "I will not agree to complete a task which is handed to me so late in the day that I will not get away from the workplace until half an hour after my official finish time."

- "When I take on a task I will speak to the boss and agree the completion time for it, and the time will be within the proper work hours of my contract."

- "I will respond immediately to any criticism of my work rate stated either privately or publicly in order to resolve inaccurate perceptions of the boss." For example, "I was working on this project for five hours as I did not take a lunch break yesterday – are you aware of this fact?"

One way to prevent the nagging is to communicate with crystal clarity about the work you are going to be able to complete and when. The boss cannot then complain on your delivery if he has agreed to the timings. When communicating these conditions, stand upright, and look the boss in the eye. Remain calm, speak slowly and deliberately, so that you are taking control of the conversation – hopefully. If the boss is adamant that a particular task has to be completed in a different timescale you may weigh up the following:

- Is the request genuine or is he 'gunning' for you?

- Will it really impact your career to say 'no' and restate – calmly – your realistic timescale?

- Can you communicate to him that the work will be of a superior quality if your timings are used?

- Will it impact the success of the company if you do it in your timescale?

- Are you prepared to work late on this occasion for any other reason?

- Show him, if necessary, a plan (perhaps a graph/flow chart) of your intended work, which might highlight where timings might have to be more flexible, or bottlenecks might occur, perhaps awaiting input from a third party, for example.

If, after considering the above, you feel you need to work in a way that is outside of the criteria you have set for your strategy you must make strong statements about getting more accurate timings on future tasks. You could drop in comments about being organised, better planning, and that you are making a special allowance on this occasion. Do not for one second allow him think you are in any way going to accept this as normal on future occasions.

Of course, there is a degree of risk in this strategy. For a start, you may find it tricky to maintain your 'superior' status when confronting the boss. You may find that colleagues will step up to the plate and take the task – for their own reasons – and this could weaken your position. Also, your boss may mark you out as a troublemaker, and this could impact your career plans or simply scupper your plans for improving the workplace environment.

But then, everything worth doing in life carries a risk. It just means that you have to be even more clever in devising the strategy. There are other actions/activities you can use that will counter these possibilities and swing things more to your advantage. For example:

Links to other boss profiles

As in dealing with the *Friend Then Foe Then Friend Again* boss, it is a good idea to change your behaviour and to behave unpredictably – not in any bad ways, but to keep everyone guessing. This will also give you more of a sense of personal control.

Here are some additional ways to make people wonder about how you are going to react or behave.

Be a shining star … occasionally

Imagine a work situation where the whole department or team is under terrible pressure. Perhaps the sales team has to pull out all the stops to swing a deal, the department has to prepare for a major presentation in a couple of days, or a manufacturer or distributor has an urgent order that needs fulfilling – in fact, any situation where your organisation has to deliver under pressure.

This is the time you offer to make the tea. This is when you get out the chocolate biscuits or order in pizza for everyone. This is the time you roll up your sleeves and get stuck into the job because it needs to be done right now or everything will be wasted. It is not normally part of your job, but this is a special occasion. If you are stunningly helpful at pivotal moments, if you are the most wonderfully supportive team player, then people will notice. At no other time will you be making the tea or taking lunch orders, because, as they say, familiarity breeds contempt. Your exceptionally helpful/supportive behaviour would become commonplace, and eventually your contribution would become invisible.

In the same way, you will intermittently shine for your boss – and thus be able to negate his objections to your independent attitude to timekeeping. In his judgment, you are difficult on many occasions, because you just can't be pressured into working late or long hours, but you balance it with outstanding moments of support and loyalty. Now he begins to see you as a bit of a maverick, not someone who can be taken for granted. When it really matters, there you are, doing what needs to be done.

How Marcus used the strategy

"I was sticking to my normal leaving time as much as possible and could see that it was driving George nuts. He really couldn't understand why I didn't respond to his threats. He would tell me that we were going to have to have 'serious words' if I didn't demonstrate more commitment. As I had now had the chance to think through how I was going to manage him, I was always ready. I told him I was totally committed but always had a reason why I couldn't stay. Or I didn't say anything at all and would just leave on time. But then I would sometimes shock him. If we had a serious problem that could impact the business, I went into hero mode.

"On one occasion there was a fuel shortage (because of the national strike by delivery tanker drivers) and we'd had terrible delays delivering the company products to distribution locations and customers. Not a single delivery had gone out for a week, when suddenly we had a delivery of fuel ourselves. All of a sudden we had the opportunity to catch up on a terrible week and get the products out. Everything needed to be done at once. All the warehouse staff were asked to work late. We had to make sure the lorries were loaded correctly. In the office we had stacks of paperwork to produce and check, we needed to liaise with the customers and distributors to make sure that they were ready to receive the products at what were going to be odd hours. It was vital to oversee the most efficient sharing of the fuel amongst our delivery fleet, and we needed to check the best delivery routes for the drivers, taking in as many drop-off points as possible.

"So we were all flat out. Of course, I was going to work late. I made sure everyone in the administration area got plenty of tea and coffee

– I persuaded one of the PAs to stay on and help. I ordered several pizzas for distribution though the office. I was running back and forwards between the warehouses and the office, making sure everyone knew what was going on. I checked all the delivery itineraries and made sure all the paperwork was in order. I got colleagues working for me and assumed a bit of authority. I was 'squeaky clean' with George, diving in and out of his office all evening to update him on how things were going. Basically, I just made myself as high profile as I could. After that evening, no one could have questioned my commitment – which was my aim. Of course, the next night I just left as normal."

Marcus worked this strategy beautifully. The point is: intermittently go the extra mile. But don't make a rod for your own back and do it too often; if you behave like a doormat, everyone will walk all over you.

Marcus continues:

"My strategy did not go unnoticed. Two days after the fuel delivery night I suggested to the other guys in my office that we should all go for a beer after work. I actually managed to get three of them to go with me! It was fantastic. We all left together and George didn't say a word. He didn't exactly leap up and cheer either, but I really felt like I had made this happen. Having the guys agreeing to leave with me and go for a drink started to change the culture in the office. They seemed relieved that someone had been able to stand up to George. It was great!

"Don't get me wrong, I didn't dislike George particularly. I just resented the way he ran the office like a bully, covering up for his own failings. I had some other plans up my sleeve, and sticking to my strategy during my two years with George probably helped a lot of people in that office."

Marcus is a great example of how confidence carried him through. What else could George have done? Unless he could have proved that Marcus was not sticking at least to his contract or was actually damaging the company, he knew there was a risk that he would have found himself with an unfair dismissal case on his hands. This boss profile would actually shrink away from a situation like that. He would be at risk of exposing his weakness and being surrounded by people who would be questioning him directly about his behaviour. The key is just to have the confidence to stand up to these bosses, in a professional calm way, and stick to it.

Marcus's other plans

Marcus referred to 'other plans' that he would use with George. Here are some examples of what he did:

The personal discussion

One was to formally ask for a meeting with George to discuss something 'personal'. It's always good if you can make this request via email or a written note. The reason being that there is no tonality in a written note, so until the meeting happens the recipient of the request has no idea to what level of seriousness the meeting will go. If you can make the meeting request at least a week in advance and not refer to it during that intervening time, the poor boss has a week to wonder what it's all about. All probing questions or attempts to move the meeting to an earlier date must be avoided. Just say you would 'rather' discuss it at your scheduled meeting.

He thinks the topic will be something personal about you, but in fact it's going to be about him.

At the meeting, you have to behave a little sheepishly. You apologise, and try to lull him into a sense of some impending confession. The confession is: that you feel terribly guilty because you are so enjoying working with XYZ Company but that the fact that he, your boss, is always so overwhelmed with work and working so late, that you would like to offer to take on some of his work. You want understand exactly what he has to do during those late hours and take some of it off him. You really want to help him, and you are willing to learn, no matter what it takes.

Again, there is some risk here, but at worst you could get some training, some extra responsibility – some more work. But remember you can still control your working hours, and keep to your agreed timescale on tasks.

Here's what is likely to happen:

To a greater or lesser degree, George may explain or justify what he does. Alternatively, he may dismiss you as not being worthy, senior or trained enough to do what he has to do. He may say the work is of a confidential nature, he may say he doesn't need your help. However, the main thing you want to establish at the meeting is that either there is some way you can help him, or that there is absolutely nothing you can do to help him. Should the topic arise at any future date, it has been noted that you have offered or are helping him.

The boss may feel threatened by your 'kind' offer. If he were to release any tasks to you he would lose some control. He cannot maintain the aura of being terribly, terribly busy and important. On the other hand it may just be that he does not want to go home to his spouse …

Express empathy

One more tip: express even more empathy. Plant the seed that he is being exploited: he's a 'mug'; his bosses must be laughing at the long hours he puts in. They think he is great because they think his long hours mean they are making money from him. Tell him it's unlikely he will get promoted because they have him exactly where they want him. They couldn't replace the number of hours he works with one other person. Suggest that he has created his own double-glazed glass ceiling … The more condescending and pitying you can make yourself sound the better. You will be blatantly patronising and he will be very irritated, and hopefully not just with you.

Your intention is to work sensible hours. In making your position stronger, his position has weakened, and in the light of offering to help, can he really continue to complain?

Join your colleagues

The *Mr Long Hours* boss is not himself a mixer. He is vulnerable because he is out of the loop and missing out on what's really going on. Lots of workplace gossip happens 'round the water cooler', in the kitchen or at the cigarette break, and these provide opportunities to enlist the support of colleagues. Joining, as Marcus did, this bullied band of employees, most of whom had not been in the world of work for very long (some had joined from school), he entered an established culture where George's behaviour was practically unquestioned. Marcus showed them how it was possible to resist his expectation of everyone to work long hours. Marcus was able to share the truth with them:

- That successful organised people make sure they can do their job in the hours allotted. He explained to them that when people are working like George they are struggling, are poor managers and unable to delegate.

- That a company needs to hire the right people to do the right jobs and that it would be difficult for George's career to progress with his current approach to work. Perhaps before he was promoted to managing director George had coped better?

Perhaps this role had overwhelmed him, or perhaps the bosses at headquarters had misguidedly promoted him, thinking his long hours were a manifestation of expertise, leadership or dedication. Perhaps they were rubbing their hands in glee thinking they had a working machine, who was expendable, and there were plenty more who would flog themselves to an early death.

Move up a level. Make contact with and build some kind of relationship with the boss's boss(es). Marcus had many reasons to be in touch with HQ. He called about delivery schedules, staff initiatives, logistical issues, and so on. He also had to discuss the continuation of certain product lines, and this gave him the opportunity to speak to George's direct boss, Doug. Marcus and Doug discovered that they shared a passion for rugby. This was now a relationship that Marcus could build on, so that, as with the *Friend Then Foe Then Friend Again* boss, he could have conversations with George that referenced Doug and would ensure that George was aware that his behaviour could in no way be 'secret' or hidden. George's office, behaviour, and world are now exposed, because he knows there is a direct channel to his bosses.

Marcus knew it was vital to create this link, also because for any further career moves he did not want the only source of information to HQ about him to be via George. Therefore, expand your network up the hierarchy. Your boss's reaction to the relationships you develop with his bosses will tell you how insecure he is. In the 'normal' world, if you are performing well, your boss should be pleased that you are impressing people across the business. After all, they hired you and that should reflect well on them.

On the other hand, a mad boss is more likely to be irritated and threatened by this relationship!

Create uncertainty

Your strategy is to establish a degree of uncertainty. The reason why you want to keep your boss on edge and wondering what you will do next is because if he ever complains about your working hours, commitment or standards, you need to remind him of your intermittent 'flashes' of superb commitment, so that he cannot generalise about your behaviour – that you always do this, or never do that. Your 'inconsistency' makes it hard for him to really pin down what's annoying him.

Other tactics

In addition to those flash moments of excellence, there are other behaviours you can perform that will keep him guessing:

- Work late for no particular reason on 'random' days.

- As well as working late, sometimes be the first to arrive in the office/shop/showroom. Don't make a big deal about it (keep your smugness to yourself). This builds on the mystique. Again (as with the Friend Then Foe profile) when you act as if you have a secret or know something no one else knows, it will all contribute to driving your boss nuts.

- Put forward unsolicited proposals, propose ideas, or create projects. This will require a little creativity on your part. You might be able to keep the work you put into this to the absolute minimum by reproducing something from a different role – perhaps an initiative you suggested or worked on for a previous employer which you can recycle for the current master. Remember that you need Doug at HQ to see your great ideas and initiatives, so make sure he finds out. Tell Doug you are working on some ideas that you really think will help George, but could he be so kind as to take a look at them first for you, because, of course, you really want to impress your boss.

Another source of good ideas and projects are those that may have been discarded in earlier times by your current organisation. For example, you may learn about an idea to allow employees to work from home, on occasion, or a new system for managing stock. It doesn't matter what it is, the main thing is that it should, as far as possible, be innovative, a little controversial and, of course, have been previously discarded by George/boss. Rework it putting in all the logistics, the costs and benefits, the technology requirement and the project plan – and release it both to your boss and to his boss. You are not actually worried about getting any plans acted upon – although that would be a bonus. The idea is to show your caring attitude concerning the future of the company (whether real or feigned) and inventiveness in suggesting radical ideas! Whatever your interest in these projects being adopted and successful, the point is to submit them. Not only do you become a dynamic go-getter, but best of all you also become a threat.

These bosses find innovative people threatening, because they fear that their inadequacies and weaknesses will be uncovered. This fear relates to the emotional investment they have already made: *If you can be successful without working long hours, it makes a complete mockery of the long hours and emotional investment I have made, over many years, to achieve this level of 'success'.* No one is happy to admit that they have wasted all those years of their life, with such limited benefit.

Be warned that there is a real chance that one of the more senior bosses may actually like your style and initiative and promote you – so be ready!

There are other ways to change your behaviour. Sometimes have very strong views on topic, and at other times act as if you have no opinion and don't care. Similarly, sometimes look very worried and be subdued, and at other times be very lively. It's all to do with making sure people listen to you. If they are never quite sure what you are going to say then they will be waiting to find out what's going on; although they may not be exactly hanging on your every word, they will be taking notice. Remember that this is not supposed to be a chore but simply a move in the right direction of regaining control.

Concluding thoughts

A company where a *Mr Long Hours* boss is in charge is sick. The sickness may be mild or it may be severe, but it is sick. The disease spreads to the families and personal lives of the employees and causes unhappiness well beyond the confines of the physical workspace.

Such bosses bully the employees until they lose sight of what is reasonable. They wonder why they have problems in their personal relationships, why they feel ill. They take too many sick days because they are so miserable and unhappy, and this only increases the pressure to do more. Bosses who can't cope tend to surround themselves with workers to justify their need for working long hours.

There is no point in tolerating such a miserable environment because in the long run no one wins. Long hours are a false economy; a company operating with tired, bullied workers does not present a good face to its customers. Any organisation that colludes with its managers to allow an environment like this will see the effect in its bottom line – profits will be affected.

Basically, and in the most professional way, you are going to undermine your boss. Yes, there is risk but if you can't change it, I would almost guarantee it's not the place you would want to stay anyway. Working against an established culture can be a tough strategy to follow. Above all you must keep going, learn to be inconsistent even if it is against your nature, and be firm in your resolve not to succumb to the pressures that will be put upon you. In other words,

- Be helpful
- Be friendly
- Be firm
- Deliver what you agree to deliver (production, hours, etc)
- Make allies out of colleagues.

As with all of the profiles your survival strategy is not a quick fix. Take your time to watch and learn. You will be a pioneer leading the change. Your strategy and strength may make the lives of many of your colleagues better. You will learn that a true manager does not 'manage' but lead – and this experience will teach you how to be a great leader.

I hope these ideas will refresh your attitude to *Mr Long Hours* so that you realise that you can make a difference and bring control back into your life. If, at the end of the day, the reward is not equal to the effort, you have still learned some great lessons. Not only will you be able to spot the profile easily in any future bosses, you will have honed your anti-*Mr Long Hours* skills and be ready for a great leadership role yourself. It's a practicable way of working smarter, just so long as you don't let one of these dinosaurs hold you back. The strategy can be exhausting. If you are getting grumpy and tired, take time out to regroup: get some distance so that you can think rationally, and update your strategy. This is the path to becoming a more efficient worker, of improving your career prospects, and of creating a more rounded and fulfilling personal life.

Managing a *Mr Long Hours* boss

Summary:

- Constantly re-prioritize your workload
    - ◆ Don't fall into the trap of spending hours doing non vital or unproductive work
    - ◆ Do not do activities other people in your organisation are supposed to be doing
    - ◆ Delegate upwards as well as to appropriate peers
- Show flashes of dedicated behaviour
    - ◆ Make the tea – but ONLY occasionally!
- Maintain your agreed work level and work hours
- Be consistent in your strategy, even when you are deliberately being inconsistent
- Make allies of colleagues and other managers
- You know how to be an efficient worker – don't get distracted!
- 'Working smarter' should be the approach, and embraced by the company

---

The old boy network is not just for the old boys

What is a network, how you build it, and why?

When you leave a company you probably never completely say goodbye. Not only do you take the learning with you to your next role, you also maintain at least some of the relationships you have forged in your jobs. Many relationships endure outside of work, especially those with the people who became your friends. But also with the other people you were working with – your 'network.' A network is a bit like a savings account. The sooner you start, the more valuable it becomes over the years – and you may find yourself saying, "I wish I'd started earlier." All you have to do is to stay in touch with people as you go through your work/business life.

Some people are naturally good at building relationships and keeping a network. In chapter nine you will meet Sir Lunchalot, the mad sales manager, who is an expert at networking. He is the sort of guy who is always able to put you in touch with someone. He has contacts everywhere, and a pocket stuffed full of dog-eared business cards. If he doesn't personally know the right person, then he knows someone who does. He is never out of work because someone always owes him a favour. He will do favours and expect them in return. Connections, information, and help, these are the power of the network.

When you leave, say goodbye, but make sure that you have a note of everyone's contact details – telephone number, email address – and occasionally be in touch. Very easy, very civilised and potentially very useful. Once you have departed, your relationship with your now ex-boss changes dramatically. You are free of him; you can speak to him in a completely different way. Make him a part of your network.

Chapter Six
Power Crazy Boss

Quick check this boss:

- Checks everything you do
- Is the ultimate 'micro manager'
- Destroys your confidence
- Crushes creativity
- Seems to enjoy exerting power
- Continuously petty
- Uses these expressions:

  "Just copy me in on that will you?"

  "Just run that by me."

  "Just let me review that."

  "I'd like to be at that meeting."

  "Let me know when you are planning to make that call."

  "Better let me handle that."

  "I'll let you know."

  "I'd do it like this."

  "We always do it this way …"

  "I'd prefer if you could just stick to doing it this way."

  "Don't change anything without letting me know."

This boss links closely to:

- *Small Business Owner*

◼ *Friend Then Foe Then Friend Again*

◼ *Fear Merchant*

◼ *Sales Manager*

If you find the expressions listed above are familiar to you, then you may have a boss who is slowly eroding your confidence, taking everything you do and doing it again (only 'better').

This is probably driving you crazy and you may suspect that he is nuts. You wonder why you bother turning up in the morning, as you know they may secretly relish the charade of 'having to do your work' or to 'cover for you'.

In this profile, we are going to look at the individual/boss who cannot go through the day without knowing about the activities of everyone under their management, not just at an overall level but down to irritating detail.

And the personality behind this behaviour? We find another frightened boss, lacking in confidence and vision. They cannot let go, find it hard to delegate, and hard to trust. They are frightened of mistakes being made which could reflect badly on them. This may be one of the most pathological of the profiles. Within an organisation, this kind of boss becomes a self-appointed checkpoint. In their eyes, they may think they are efficient and caring, but this may be covering a deep-seated fantasy that they are the only person capable of making the right decision. Having a conscience as clear as crystal, they conveniently forget that they ever made a mistake or ever went through any sort of learning curve in the past. Most likely the opposite is true.

They fail to recognise that the only way people truly grow, and the only way they can develop the talent that they have hired, is to let them learn by making some mistakes. People need guidance; they do not need their confidence crushed by the constant interference of another person.

As time goes by, people working under these conditions lose their confidence and become increasingly worried about making mistakes. As a result, they naturally, by default, refer to this boss more and more. The profile is self-fulfilling. *Power Crazy* bosses believe their own story that they need to constantly check up on people. They can justify this thinking because people do keep referring to them and checking they are doing the right thing. This they smugly feed off, enhancing their self-created illusion of power. As this self-importance grows their mental space decreases through fear: "How would this organisation manage without me?" they think – heedless of the work that entails, and of the damage it is doing to the business. Not only are processes slowing down but more importantly people are giving up. They produce increasingly poorer work; a vicious circle is in operation. They are crushed because, "What's the point? Whatever I do, the boss will tell me how it should be done ... their way."

The business is slowed and deadened by the *Power Crazy* boss. Nothing happens without their OK; the workforce is subdued, creativity goes unacknowledged and unrewarded, and innovation dies.

The learning curve for any individual within a new role is like nurturing an inquisitive child or an exotic hot-house flower. If you cannot give it the space or environment to grow it will die before it reaches its true potential. Employees in this situation can never deliver the best value for the organisation. Employees do not need constant criticism; they do need encouragement and support and the space to express themselves. The demonstration of leadership is through encouraging people to find their own path to success, not by haranguing them when they are learning through their mistakes.

Confidence comes when you know that whatever you do will work out in some way or another. Confidence comes from being OK with the unknown, the unexpected. If, as an employee, you can only operate by asking your boss for permission, your lack of confidence will show when, for example, you are dealing with customers face-to-face in challenging situations. There are times when you need to do something which may not be part of your organisation's rules or processes, something your micro-management boss would not condone, and where you would be told you had done something wrong. If, because of lack of support, you do not have the confidence to respond in an unorthodox yet appropriate way, you could lose your company a customer and advocate.

For example, callcentre employees take a lot of stick. Their work is controlled and monitored minute by minute, keystroke by keystroke throughout the day. The processes are often restrictive and remove any chance of independent action from the individual.

No wonder that the general public who have to contact a company through a call centre begin to treat the staff like malfunctioning machines! The processes dictate that they practically behave like that!

The 'boss' in a busy utility company call centre may be some kind of remote management team who have installed processes that take all power away from the frontline staff. Losing one or two customers is hardly noticed by the company, but bad mouthing, directly and through detractors' websites, can swiftly give the company a terrible reputation for customer service. That's when companies do start to take notice.

Carl's story

This case study recounts the experience of Carl.

Carl was 22 when he started work in a call centre for a well-known utility company based in the North West of England. Although he accepted it was not a major career decision (he had studied photography and fully intended making that his chosen path – he was just looking for the right organisation to join), he had enjoyed customer-facing roles in the past. As a teenager he had worked in a local cycle shop and occasionally as a barman. In both these former roles, he had enjoyed serving people, helping them make choices and solving problems. The idea of a 'proper' customer service role, with the chance to resolve customer issues and being able to use his naturally positive attitude working at the call centre, seemed like the perfect interim position.

Almost immediately he realised that the 'system' precluded any chances for him to exercise his natural, helpful personality.

It went further. If he had ever decided to go 'off script' there would be consequences. The system enforced a route from which you could not stray, mandatory fields had to be filled, and responses were supplied to practically all enquiries. It was just not possible to take a customer enquiry or problem and try to solve it; the system would report any deviation, record all the conversations and potentially alarm bells would ring!

Carl did not enjoy the work because he was restricted by the control of that distant unseen management team who had decided the most efficient way to deal with customers. His role was to simply process them in the way the system they had designed dictated, with the human interface severely restricted, and with no more purpose than to fulfil the organisation's advertising boast, that their customers could call and "speak to 'real people' not a voice recording". However, Carl did not feel like a 'real person' for long. He described it as a soul-destroying experience:

> *"I could not do 'the right thing' because the system often gave me no option to satisfy the customer. The process offered me only compulsory answers, tick boxes and drop-down menus. I could not be the helpful person I wanted to be; the system manipulated the entire interaction with the customer."*

Carl became very frustrated with the work and was pleased that he would not have to be there for long. He described a typical experience, which many people who have worked in this environment will recognise, that of not having the power to help even though you want to and are perfectly able to.

> *"A lady was put through to me to ask about her bill. There had been an error on the paperwork – her bill stated she owed £1,000, but she believed it was incorrect and should only be £100. 'There is an extra '0' on the figure' she insisted. She was very distressed – she could not pay the bill as it was and was really worried about having her supply cut off. I was able to look at the details of the lady's account. I could see that for the previous ten bills she had been charged £100 and that she had always paid on time. I really wanted to tell her not to worry and that it was obviously a mistake. I wanted to fix the problem and send out a correct new bill."*

But the system process meant Carl could not solve the problem.

> *"I effectively had to say things that meant 'this organisation does not trust you, even though you have been a customer for five years'. It was*

awful. All I could do was make a note on the system. I had to ask her to call another number to arrange for a new meter reading to be taken so that the figures could be checked. She was very unhappy that we could not just resolve the problem straight away. I know there could be times when people try to get out of paying, but bear in mind the company could always check the usage and amend a future bill. There would be so little risk in making this customer happy; all I could do was add to her stress. Things like this used to happen all the time. In the end you give up trying to be too helpful or imaginative, the system takes over."

In this case, Carl had no power to rectify a simple error that his organisation had made. The distressed customer had to go through another lengthy interaction, possibly with another disenfranchised callcentre employee to complain about the issue, and sort out the process to rectify it. The mad distant managers who had implemented a rigid solution for dealing with these pesky customers were probably congratulating themselves on the speedy process they had created, the fact that it eliminated mistakes, captured all the essential information, and prevented agent error. By taking all decisions and options away from the person involved, they believed they had ensured their organisation would be secure in the future. Brilliant! No problem there then.

But if they would take the time to examine the consequence of their actions, of effectively neutering the agents, perhaps even they might reconsider. For example, how much more time and expense is now involved with the issue that Carl encountered? The customer has to call back, the issue has to be discussed a second time, someone from the company will have to go as soon as possible and reread the meter. The cost of this activity is borne by the utility company, who will be paying another agent to process this interaction, effectively for the second time.

Imagine a centre of empowered agents who can make decisions, who could go off script and generally be themselves? Would it really be worse than the current set-up? Would there be an opportunity to delight thousands of jaded customers, who would be only too willing to tell their friends about this differentiating experience?

So next time you phone a call centre, think about the person on the other end of the line. They almost certainly will have script from which they are not permitted to deviate. Every conversation, every keystroke is recorded; every minute of their time when they are not talking to a customer has to be accounted for. In addition, they are told to 'have a smile' in their voice! Could you work like this?

I can only imagine how frustrating this way of working must be. How do you think the agent feels? What do you think the customers feel? For millions of workers poor processes implemented by ignorant bosses are causing frustration and bottlenecks (for employees and customers). Many misguided organisations have lost their way in integrating people with processes, and as a consequence use neither to the best advantage.

This example seeks to show the crushing effect that over-monitoring can have, whether by a boss or a process designed by a boss. Whether it's a department with an overzealous manager, or a shop floor, if you cannot bring your own personality, style and experience to the role, it will end up depleting your energy and eroding your confidence. There is no way you can give your best; why try any harder than reaching the minimum requirement? And because it will not be fun, it will affect all the people you are interacting and communicating with, be they colleagues or just as importantly, customers.

Strategies for the Power Crazy Boss

You will be disappointed in my lack of truly creative thoughts for emerging from or changing the call centre environment, but I do have some.

- Look upon working in a service industry as a life-experience that will hold you in good stead for your possible future in management. It will certainly teach you a lot about tolerance and consideration for those who find themselves in such positions. Perhaps every potential manager should spend time working in a call centre, waiting at table, serving behind the bar, or as a hospital orderly, in order to realise these insights. Whatever the environment, watch, listen and learn, not just about the equipment and the systems, but about people. Find out about what works when it comes to motivating employees.

Hopefully if you are in the role already it's not your life's career, but as a student or for some other reason temporarily. The national figures for staff turnover in call centres would certainly support this hope.

- Become the call centre manager. This is not as wild as it sounds. Given the staff churn figures in this industry, it's not impossible to end up as a manager of a reasonably-sized team in around 18 months. Just stay and do a half decent job. Don't worry, you will get there by default – everyone else will leave. It's entirely feasible. Then you will start to have the opportunity to influence the working conditions.

This learning environment is somewhat similar to the Small Business Owner profile.

- As the trend currently sits with the off-shoring of call centre operations there is an opportunity for setting up an operation of your own, that will deliver those intangible benefits which some organisations have already found significantly impact the customer experience – i.e. local knowledge, local accent, cultural understanding. There is a well-known business ethos that says, "When the herd (business community) moves, don't follow but head in the other direction." In other words, the next opportunity isn't where everyone is heading now. The requirement for specialised out-sourced services is alive and well and based in your home country. Will the next new, specialised, top quality call centre be yours?

Strategies for the smaller team

You are in the office, and for the umpteenth time your boss is telling you that the slides in your PowerPoint presentation don't generate the right story. What do you do, apart from walking out (not recommended), or shouting at them: "Don't you know there is more than one way to skin a cat?!" (also not recommended).

Could you apply the strategies suggested for the previous types of boss? Well, for a start, you do need to find a way to regain control, but first, you need to step back, get some space to notice what's happening and to plan your strategy. This will initially stop you trying so hard. If everything you produce is criticised and it's driving you nuts, then give yourself a break. You already know that whatever you produce is not going to satisfy them so 'trying harder' is not going to work. In a calm, relaxed state of mind your memory will work better, and you will be able to construct the outline plans for a strategy to deal with this power mad boss. When you are feeling comfortable, think, and trust your instincts.

Check your personal standards. If you know deep down that what you are producing is up to standard, and you are willing to stand by it, then carry on doing it. After all, you are in your present role because someone decided you were suitable, based on your previous successes. Since you started this job, recall what you have learned. Notice how you have already incorporated your learning into who you are right now. Now is the time to be diligent – but stop worrying! Once you are feeling more comfortable in yourself, you will be better able to deal with your boss's reactions and conversations.

Make changes to the letter, but nothing more

One possible scenario goes like this:

> The conversation begins with the boss saying that he wants to change this word or that image – to you an irrelevant detail – and you find that what you had considered to be your work has suddenly lost its integrity. Never mind. You agree to make the changes they have 'suggested'.

Now, what do you actually do? Well, the simplest strategy is to only make the changes they have requested, and give it back to them. The point is that your boss is wasting your time because whatever you produce they are going to change anyway. Your overarching strategy is: Don't waste your time. There are other things you can find to do; other activities in your working day will bring you much greater reward. What would be a better use of your time? Could you be networking, introducing yourself or talking to your boss's boss? Should you be spending the time looking for another job?

But you can do more. You are still going to make changes, but you have a bigger game-plan. You hold in mind one overall intention: You are going to arrange for your *Power Crazy* boss – whether in an office, or on a building site, shop, or factory floor – to do your work. It's the yin-yang theory: either you are frustrated on a daily basis with their petty interfering and fight against it, or you release your annoyance and go with the flow.

Let them suggest, correct, enhance, and amend your work as much as they like. As long as this piece of work is of good quality, instead of getting mad, make sure that it has your name all over it. For example, if it involves written text, put your name in a header or footer as well as on the title page. If it is a drawing, sign it; if it's a presentation, tell everyone about *your* presentation personally. In other words, if you want to be associated with this excellent piece of work, make sure other people know it's yours.

Use your boss's fault to your own advantage. If they have rejected your input on so many occasions that you know you can never deliver what they want, then let them work for you. Excel in the areas where you do bring value and let this area go. Accept their input and in a parasitic way suck their brains dry of any knowledge or expertise. Use the effort they are willing to put into your work so that it enhances your contribution to your advantage. I am assuming that their amendments do actually add value and get results, even if they don't quite fit your style.

Whatever it is, the first strategy is to distance yourself from the problem, let go of the emotional stuff, and generally keep your opinions to yourself. Don't bad mouth anyone in public (whatever your inclination) as it will act against you. Then develop your proactive strategy by utilising your boss's 'faults' to your advantage. Then you can deal with the issues in a more head-on way by starting to steer your boss into a position where you bring more control back in your work world.

Remember to forget

Another way of dealing with a *Power Crazy* boss who is constantly correcting the work that you are doing is to gradually cut them out of the loop. Previously, you have been nagged into the habit of going to them to check your communications. Whenever the boss knows that you are about to communicate (submit a report or letter, give a presentation, and so on) you have been told to "Run it by me first". Now you are somehow going to 'forget' to do this.

Here's what you do. At first, you are testing the waters, so start gently 'forgetting' to check things with them, preferably on the not-so-vital low-level stuff that you are 100% confident with, and notice the response you get. Do you need to justify these 'slips'? Perhaps you do: there was a deadline, the boss was so busy, unavailable, and so on. If you must, you can make excuses. But you will be stronger if you don't. You agree: "You're right. No, I didn't." Again, this can be part of your behaving differently strategy. Stand your ground, never explain nor justify. Act as if this is the way you always do things, and look puzzled if this is challenged. If the boss is annoyed, you could, for the first few times at least, apologise, "I'm sorry. I didn't run that one past you." You could also adapt your tonality to suggest a sense of 'that was so trivial', 'hardly worth your time', and so on. At first you may exasperate the boss as they begin to feel they are losing some of their control. As long as you make these changes gradually, as long as you don't cause a major cock-up, the boss will not really be able to complain. The next stage is to start forgetting to apologise. You will also feel your power returning as you refuse to play their game and 'educate' them away from checking the more routine stuff. It's a weaning process. This will work if done carefully and consistently. Maintain your professional status, and be helpful and reliable in all other activities.

Then you are going to up the stakes. Continue the process with the higher-level project work. Don't ask them for help or input unless you need it and tell them this is how you are going to do it. This could be a high-risk strategy, but if you are sure of your content then go for it. With this profile of boss you are unlikely to find that you can sustain this role from a professional point of view, unless you evolve. If you are constantly undermined and cannot see any improvement you may have to explore alternative employment, but at least you will now have the experience to recognise the traits.

Say it straight

There is an aligned strategy here if you have an otherwise reasonable relationship with your boss but are just exasperated with their constant checking and changing. Tell them how frustrated you are with their habit and point out the advantages for them of not having to check your work all the time. Promise them you will ask them if you need help. For the first couple of instances you could even fake needing their help to make them feel more secure. At first they will be resistant. It may be possible as an interim step to agree a simple review process. For example, you produce the work and have an agreement that says that one review is part of the process and no more. The review can amend any technical detail or accuracy issue but not the style, language or sequence of the work. This however will be very difficult to achieve unless the boss has acknowledged that they need to let go, or can see the benefits of doing so.

The 'glass ceiling' ploy

You have tried to take the control back from them. You have ignored the request to let them constantly review your work. You have upped the stakes to the more high level work. You have asked them to agree to not interfere unless you ask them to. Are they still trying to check all your work?

You now have to take the gloves off – but in the nicest possible way. It might be better to have this conversation over a beer or after hours, or as part of conversation about work in general rather than highlighting it as a topic for a special meeting. You know your own boss best, so you decide the timing and context.

You are going to have to find a way of explaining how they are creating a glass ceiling for themselves. How do you do this without them feeling you are threatening them? This boss has to be diverted from his internal gazing. You want them to stop concentrating on you. Here are some options:

- Have they ever thought about how they will get to the next stage? Can you create a hunger in them for the next step up the ladder?

- Have they thought about succession planning? Can you give them some ideas about how they could make a name for themselves with their bosses? Can you tell them how they might do this?

- Do they fancy so-and-so's job? Do they think they are better than the people who manage them? Do they realise that the company is limiting them because they present an 'indispensable' image? The company can't promote them from their role because they are so wrapped up in sorting out the details of their current position. They need to look outside the problems they deal with at the tactical level and present strategic solutions for their company. They need to want to shine and show their bosses how they have ideas about how to improve the company. How could they improve profitability, customer loyalty, productivity, anything else?

It's a tough conversation. How far you can go, and at what speed, will depend on how well you know them. It may help to introduce the ideas slowly. You have to describe how true leaders don't get bogged down in the minutiae of every little detail of the business, but take a strategic overview. If they don't look to rise above checking every communication in their workplace, they will remain in that position indefinitely.

If your boss is impressed by research or outside authorities, then you could direct them to material such as Pfeffer & Sutton (2006) in which they raise the question: "How can a leader tell when it is best to get out of the way, or best to start hanging around where his or her people work, asking questions, and giving people advice and feedback?"[3]

They offer some basic rules for bosses: "if you know less about the work than the people you are managing, get out of the way unless you want to learn something from them." And if you want your people to be creative, you have to allow them to make mistakes, because that's how they learn. If you hover over them, constantly monitoring their progress, it's highly likely that you will start focusing on the negatives rather than the positives. As David Kelley, the boss of IDEO says, "I just hire some smart people and get out of the way."

Mistakes

Find out your boss's attitude towards mistakes.

- What is the real impact of a mistake?
- Have they ever made a mistake?
- How did they learn?

---

3. Jeffrey Pfeffer and Robert I Sutton (2006) *Hard Facts: Dangerous Half-truths and Total Nonsense: Profiting from Evidence-Based Management,* Harvard Business School Press, page 209.

You may ask them "How do you expect me to learn if you don't allow me to make mistakes?" If they say "I'm 'saving' you from making mistakes," you reply "But I need to see the *consequences* of my mistakes, and you are preventing me from doing that." You could then agree to explore the consequences of making mistakes. The mad boss may panic at this point as you will be discussing the very essence of their fears but alternatively you may find that this discussion dissipates them. Either way it is a positive communication which will enable you to start to really understand each other's position, and form a platform from which you can potentially move to a more comfortable working environment.

Your options

Here are your options for the *Power Crazy* boss in the small team environment:

- Let them get on with it and benefit from their fault.
- Face it head-on and try and just start 'forgetting' to check with them.
- Tell them how frustrating it is for you and agree a minimum process with them for checking you work, if necessary.
- Communicate to them regarding the impact of creating a glass ceiling.
- If possible, discuss the issues and articulate each other's fears as a basis for moving forward.

By ignoring their requests to interfere with your communications, for example, you will show them that the world does not fall apart just because they haven't checked your work. By doing this with irritating regularity they will become desensitised to the process. They have to stop feeling anxious about you doing things on your own. When you have started to successfully implement this first strategy, that is the time to start having the conversations about how much the boss has to be involved.

You need to manage your boss. Agree the process together. Then with that in place (even if not working) you have to get vicious (you might call this 'honest') and tell them he is going to be a failure if he doesn't change his style. And then in the best 'good-cop bad-cop' style, while they are contemplating their failed career, tell them how you can help by taking some of the detail off their plate. Even offer to check the work of other employees for them.

If they are listening, and in conciliatory mood, this could be the best result of all. That is, if they still feel that all work needs checking try and get them to implement a peer-to-peer checking process. No one is as harsh as a colleague when it comes to telling you what is wrong with your work! But you also get the chance to check theirs. This has several benefits:

- The boss can be aloof from the process and not bogged down in it.

- The boss is free to do the boss things they should be doing.

- A peer-to-peer-process creates excellent standards, as the team/ department becomes responsible for its results. It can become a team building environment. Make the criticism process a blame free learning experience.

If he still won't play ball …

Suppose that your *Power Crazy* boss still won't let go. Is there anything else you can do? There is now a need to book the 'personal' meeting with them. Remember how you did that for with *Mr Long Hours*? (page 71) Ask for a meeting to discuss a personal issue. Make sure there is as long as possible between the meeting and the time you ask for it (ideally at least a week). Refuse to discuss the topic with them in the meantime. You want them to think it's really serious; because this time it will be.

In the meeting you may get emotional, but that's fine, it will only enforce just how seriously you feel about the subject. Ask them challenging questions. Making them face up to your issues because you are not happy is not easy if they have already refused to make changes with the strategies you have suggested so far. What are you going to ask?

- Do you remember why you hired me?

- What are the things you like about the work I do?

- What do you like, or admire about me, as a person?

Try not to raise your voice while asking these questions, stay steady: You want him to give honest answers, but this is not about trying to initiate a friendship. You need to stay objective; you want them to get beneath the surface and discover what's real for them. You want to make them think about the things that they do like about you. Are they saying they made a mistake in hiring you? You want them to recognise and appreciate your contribution, to say some positive things about you. Show some examples of your work – the good stuff – and ask them what they are really worried about? Tell them if they insist on reworking all your work that you will let them. They need a reality check on the great staff they have picked.

You could also ask them to put themselves your position. Can they imagine what it's like to be continuously questioned about their work? Ask them to recall their own experiences with their various bosses.

If nothing more, get this conversation to be the starting point of agreeing some new boundaries for their reviewing process. Together you will agree a process for them to release their grip on you. You are going to regain your sanity.

You have to be the real adult here. They are the scared one. They are scared you will make a mistake that could reflect badly on them. They are scared that they will be superfluous. They do not know how to delegate. What are they going to do? Do they have the quality to make the next grade or is their strategy to remain successful and indispensable at the level they're at? They may think they can't be better and be scared to put themselves out on a limb, letting go of their interference 'comfort blanket'. So be patient with them …

Let them know that your success will only reflect well on them.

The strategies for this profile are simple but some of the toughest in this book. You need your boss to make some steps towards you. Sometimes these bosses need to be reined in because they just have never been told about their faults before. It can be a bit of a shock for them to find out that their interfering is not only unwelcome but causing stress in the workforce.

Rather than seeing your constructive comments as a threat, impress upon your boss the advantages it will bring for them.

Top managers across the world agree that to be successful you need to hire the best people you can, in fact, hire people better than themselves. Never take on anyone who does not aspire to do your job. Unless you have succession planning you cannot move up yourself. You build quality, success and intelligence into your team – so use it!

How far you can take this will depend on carefully judging the conversations with your boss. You need them to know you are not happy about the situation. You will need to connect with them at as many levels as possible.

Managing a *Power Crazy* boss

Summary

- Remember to forget – wean them from their checking
- If they resist – use their fault to your advantage, it frees you for other activity
- Show them that they are creating the illusion of being 'indispensable'. Ask them: "Do they really want that role forever?"
- Encourage them to reference outside authorities
- Remind them that they once made mistakes – and that it's only by making mistakes that people learn, and it's not the end of the world!
- Remind them why they hired you in the first place
- Suggest other methodologies such as peer-to-peer monitoring
- Be patient and communicate simply – they're scared

Chapter Seven
No Power Boss

Quick check this boss:

- Friendly
  - ◆ Joins all the team events
- Appeasing
- Weak, ineffectual
  - ◆ Wants to be your 'friend'
  - ◆ Fails to intervene when needed
- Scared of some employees
  - ◆ Afraid of demanding results
  - ◆ Afraid of being disliked

This boss links to:

- *I Hired You, Now I Hate You*

This boss may not be so friendly but they abandon you in your moment of need

- *Friend Then Foe Then Friend Again*

In his lucid, friendly moments he can fail to act decisively

The universal excuse

You may find yourself in a situation where you have been asked to do something that you really do not want to do, can't do, or are not prepared to do. Instead of making an excuse which is an attempt to justify your non-compliance for whatever reason, a more efficient way is to use the universal unassailable excuse.

The universal unassailable excuse is the excuse you give your boss, colleague, or anyone else, to let them know you will not be doing what they have requested. You tell them you cannot do it for 'personal reasons'.

I first came across this little gem in my recruitment days, when I saw my senior clients ducking out of important meetings, not taking posts they were offered or generally getting out of anything they didn't fancy.

They would simply say, "I can't make that meeting I'm afraid, it's because of personal reasons." And that would be the end of it. The beauty of this statement/response is that 99% of people will not question it.

Say it in a slightly 'serious' voice and it's nearly guaranteed, no one will pry, no one will question. People, although they will wonder what's going on, are almost universally bound by an etiquette that will not permit them to probe.

As with other tactics suggested in this book, the way to get the best results is to use a mix-and-match approach for your strategies. You cannot overuse this excuse. No one will take it seriously if you say it three times a week – just like some of the other strategies. Use it when you really need it, for example like when you need the 'sickie' day.

Characteristics/profile of the No Power Boss

The *No Power* boss is a completely ineffectual individual and is almost the opposite of the *Power Crazy* profile. On occasion you could find yourself practically begging this boss to make changes, and find that they consistently fail to take action on the various issues in the workplace.

This person:

■ is insecure, they harbour a deep desire to be liked

■ is unable to handle/shies away from any type of confrontation

■ feels that if they ask for something to be done and it doesn't happen they are unsure how to enforce it

■ lacks assertiveness

■ doesn't want to rock the boat

This is the boss who may ignore a safety issue because they feel they haven't the authority to make a fuss within the organisation, to request or demand action. They may have asked an employee to fix something and the instruction may have been ignored.

This boss allows issues, disputes or inequalities between colleagues to go unresolved because they are frightened or unable to discipline an employee. They may not be able to manage a situation where one person in the team is bullying another. They are cowards, they are scared of not being liked and they are scared of confrontation. They think that the way to get people to do things is to get them to like you.

Another version of this is a boss who has been given the title of a boss but in fact has *No Power*. There may be issues that need sorting but the 'boss' in this case has not the funds, resources or recognised authority to make the necessary changes. This is also another version of unacceptable management. They just do not have the power you think they have. They have the title but no change in their level of authority has been implemented. They can be the cause of misery, discontent and anger, have no way to fix the problems and are worse than useless.

Then there is the *No Power* boss who has all the power, the authority to make changes and implement new process, discipline staff and remove troublemakers – but won't.

I came across it during a course on personality profiling, where it was referred to as the 'Jesus profile'. These bosses find it very difficult not to see things from the other point of view. They can be a deeply emotional person, projecting their personal response to situations on to others, not realising that it will not necessarily feel the same to them. This person is constantly struggling internally. They think through every action, they may take every decision to the nth degree and therefore end up doing nothing. They can always see the multiple results of every action they could take. They want to be all things to all men. They seek not to upset anyone, to offer unbounded consideration and empathy. They make allowance for every conceivable behaviour and find it a real challenge to exact discipline.

Occasionally, these characters can make great leaders – people are attracted by their even-handedness and generous spirits. They can also be loathed for their passive approach.

This boss cannot take action before all the pieces of his company jigsaw have been fitted together – and this never happens. In their head they want to lead people; they wholeheartedly believe that people have goodness in them and that all they have to do is encourage and expose that goodness.

This boss is yoked to the management mantra that they are there to serve the employees, to facilitate their success whatever the circumstances. If they have to let an employee go you would think from the way they handle it that they were making their own sister redundant. They have a big heart, are full of emotion and dedication, but sometimes blind to the undermining behaviour of disruptive people.

Although having such qualities can be desirable, in the extreme, when it comes to dealing with confrontational or emotional work situations, this personality is too idealistic. These qualities can lead to the over-analysis of situations (referred to in business circles as 'analysis paralysis') and an ensuing lack of action or direction. Such bosses never show favouritism; even to their favourites they are scrupulously fair. It is extremely frustrating to work for such a boss because of their lack of willingness to take action, their inability to know when they are being taken advantage of, and their failure to see the misery they are creating as a consequence of their lack of intervention. For example, failing to deal with, or even accept that bullying is occurring, despite the obvious unhappiness. Because of this experience employees find they feel let down and demotivated.

These are difficult situations to deal with, yet for a boss doing nothing can not be an option. However, their ingrained style of equal treatment for all and lack of strength to act in such frustrating circumstances is a recipe for trouble.

On a one-to-one level this type of *No Power* boss may actually be a very pleasant person. You may get on well with them. Your relationship, for a while, at least, may seem to be one of the best you have ever had with a boss. After a time, though, you realise that they cannot exert their authority, that they seem unable to understand how to use the power at their disposal, that they live in a perpetual state of inertia or paralysis – and all your efforts to get things done through this boss dissipate into thin air.

As you can see, the *No Power* boss is out in the workplace under several different guises. Of all the bosses they may be the best to work with from some points of view, but when you need support, leadership and strength, shouldn't you be able to expect it, at least in some small dose, from your boss?

Suzanne's story

Suzanne worked in a small bookshop and stationers in a quiet market town in the South-East of the UK. Her husband worked for a major insurance company and, as their children had all now left home, they were looking to enjoy a relaxed life in their home town. Suzanne needed the job in the bookshop in order to pay off the remaining debts from putting their kids through college and also to fund her hobby of breeding miniature Yorkshire terriers.

The problem she experienced grew over a period of two years. This story demonstrates the misery wrought by the *No Power* boss.

Working with a difficult colleague

Suzanne found herself with a *No Power* boss in the bookshop.

Her area manager, Jo, was fairly young for the role but had been promoted as a result of long service: she had worked for the company for seven years, having started while still at school as a Saturday girl aged 16. So at the ripe old age of 23, Jo knew more about the practicalities of the job than many of her more mature peers. The company had promoted her because of her knowledge about the company processes, the products, and, of course, she could pass on her expertise on window displays, promotions, store layout and the book business in general. At one level, she was a very useful asset to the company.

Suzanne enjoyed getting to know her manager, Jo. After only a few weeks in her new role she had decided that Jo was one of the most friendly bosses she had ever known. Jo made life pleasant at the branch as she took time to explain how she wanted things to be, and Suzanne enjoyed working with a lovely young boss, who was easygoing and approachable. However, not all the staff in the branch had the same opinion of Jo.

From the start, Suzanne found it difficult dealing with Doreen who had been with the company for more years than anyone could remember. Now, her retirement was not far off. Doreen did not hide the fact that she resented the lively young area manager. However, she directed her venom at Suzanne, in the form of negative and obstructive behaviour – but only when Jo was not around to witness it.

This kind of situation is quite common. One person thinks they deserve more in the way of recognition, and cannot understand why they have not been promoted. Although this case is set in a bookshop, you could think of Doreen as the overlooked, long-serving head of department who gripes about her lot and undermines the newly appointed shiny, young, new manager. At this late stage, it is impossible to say whether the negative demeanour, sarcastic and uncalled for nasty comments started before or after the first time she had been passed over for recognition. We do know that not even a branch managership had come her way – so it was a bit of a chicken-and-egg story as to which had come first. Either way she seemed to be constantly bloody-minded and made no effort to hide this from her colleagues.

It went further: she gave friends who visited the shop discounts to which they were not entitled. She thought nothing of talking to friends, in person or on the phone, for hours at time. She occasionally 'lost' books of gift tokens or gave the wrong change but never expressed any apology or remorse. She complained about whatever task she was requested to do and generally was unpleasant to everyone, but especially Suzanne.

On top of resenting the fact that she was now approaching the end of her working life she resented the relationship between Suzanne and Jo.

Jo had arranged a rota of staff who worked in turn to be the keyholder in each branch. The keyholder was the person responsible for opening and closing the branch each day and it was a task only allotted to the most trusted and reliable of the staff. The keyholder pool consisted of three staff all of whom were full-time. Doreen, who had recently taken to being a part-time worker, did not qualify as a keyholder. Due to the flat organisational structure within each branch, the keyholder at any time was also the temporary supervisor and would receive instructions from Jo regarding any arrangements, promotions, or other details about running the store for that period. Because of the type of staff it employed, the company found that having a number of people taking turns to be 'in charge' was beneficial in that the effect of staff absences or turnover carried less impact on the business. Also, the knowledge required to run the business in the absence of the manager was distributed to a wider employee base.

What was supposed to happen was: Jo would breeze in, allot tasks to the keyholder, and generally update everyone. She would make suggestions on displays and promotions and disappear on to the next branch in her patch.

What she continually failed to do was to sort out the problems Doreen was causing. She listened attentively to her staff trying to tell her about Doreen's disruptive and upsetting behaviour but did nothing about it. Once or twice she spoke to Doreen, but it was obvious that her friendly style was ineffectual with such a gorgon. Jo would ask 'how things were going' and Doreen would respond by being humble and conciliatory. But as soon as Jo left she would revert to her normal behaviour.

Without the manager on site, Doreen became evil. In additional to her poor work style and inappropriate behaviour, she would also act in ways which distressed her colleagues. After months of not pulling her weight in the shop, taking breaks as and when she pleased, turning up late and flat out refusing to do even the smallest tasks, the staff, who were frustrated with lack of response to their pleas to Jo, were becoming unhappy. Suzanne was particularly affected and on occasion had found she had taken days off sick rather than go to work to face Doreen. Doreen had taken a particular dislike to Suzanne.

One particular stunt that Doreen liked to pull – guaranteed to upset everyone and ruin the day for all her colleagues – was to wait until the shop was very busy and then just suddenly announce to her colleagues that she was going to take a break. Sometimes Doreen would do this in response to a minor event such as a question or simple request. Making the most of the customers in the shop – her captive audience – she would start to shout at the selected colleague being abusive and angry: "Why are you always picking on me? You know I need a break! It's not fair! I just wanted to have a sit down for five minutes! I am telling you I can't take much more of this!" and so on. She always reinforced her words with shouting and shrieking bordering on crying – her way of causing the maximum embarrassment and discomfort to the poor member of staff who had made the original request.

Doreen created such scenes as often as she could get away with them. Her plan was to promote the illusion in front of customers that she was a persecuted victim. It would have been laughable if it were not so humiliating for the particular colleague she had picked on. It might have tolerable if she had done this less frequently, but as it was, she had her colleagues on tenterhooks: they never knew when Doreen would flare. Living with this kind of tension was disruptive and made everyone else unhappy.

She was merciless with Suzanne! Suzanne realised she just couldn't go on taking this abuse from Doreen and, after a helpful conversation with her husband, finally decided she had nothing to lose by confronting her. The fateful day arrived when another scene un-rolled during which Doreen singled out Suzanne as the butt of her tirade. Suzanne was upset and emotional but, forcing herself, demanded that she and Doreen go and 'have it out' in the staff room.

Suzanne and Doreen argued about the behaviour. Suzanne was shaking with anger but she could not get a satisfactory response out of Doreen. Doreen knew her power and knew there was no point in arguing. She had achieved what she had wanted: to upset and disrupt the group.

What do you do in this situation? There is conflict between colleagues: one is not pulling their weight, bullying others or generally not contributing; the other is trying to do a good job, which includes looking after the customers. In this scenario – which could occur in almost any similar work situation – some kind of higher authority is needed to resolve the issue and set boundaries. So naturally, just like Suzanne, you turn to your manager. That is the person who will help you, surely?

Your boss lets you down

Suzanne is in a job she generally likes and feels comfortable with. She likes her boss and other colleagues but is being bullied and upset on a regular basis to the point where she has had several days off sick and is feeling depressed and stressed. She does not want to leave, she wants the situation sorted. What can she do?

However, Jo, the manager, is ineffectual and weak. In fact she is as scared as hell. There must be many bosses who, not having the training or maturity, fail to manage because they are simply afraid of being disliked. Jo did not believe she could discipline Doreen because she may have shouted or been abusive back to her. She was not strong or confident enough to do this. But being nice did not work; nor did creating a pleasant relationship

with Doreen in the hope that she would become more agreeable and bid-
dable.

> Jo had already asked her bosses about how to deal with the situ-
> ation, as there had been a series of difficulties, but these higher
> authorities were unable to offer any practical solution. Jo's par-
> ticular manager took the stance that Jo must cope with it herself
> because if she brought in other people to deal with the situation it
> would undermine her in the future. Head office told Jo that they did
> not want to make Doreen redundant. It would be a very expensive
> exercise given the amount of time Doreen had been with the com-
> pany. Head office also said that unless Jo had initiated and followed
> a thorough disciplinary process they could not fire her. They knew
> that Doreen was just the sort of employee to start legal proceedings
> if she thought there were any gaps in their process. And any way, it
> would not be that long till she retired…

Jo's situation was not straightforward. She too was being let down by her
bosses and the end result was the misery in their workplace.

Finding a workable strategy

The following strategy deals with the problem rather than the problem
boss. However, it will still work in terms of increasing your happiness at
work, and will also educate the 'problem boss'. You will need to liaise with
and organise your fellow sufferers to get a result.

You are going to discover ways to counter and diffuse the impact of your
Doreen. Try to use the campaign against this person to strengthen the
bonds between the rest of the team. Even though not everyone feels the
same, you will need to enlist as much help as you can.

You know that Jo is useless in this situation but, even so, you need her help.
If possible, arrange to meet your supporting colleagues off site. In this scenario, all of the people had personally suffered at the hands of Doreen so
it was easy to rally support.

There are some risks of which to be aware. In a larger organisation, colleagues who have not experienced the bullying may wonder why you are arranging an off-site meeting to discuss a fellow worker:

■ Is this the only route you can take?

■ You don't want to be viewed as bullies, or vigilantes yourselves

In a bigger organisation with a larger, more supportive and distributed management team things are less likely to escalate to this level. You should, in the larger company, have access to a formal procedure, and a personnel or HR department, who will have the tools to help you deal with this situation, however ineffectual your boss. Perhaps it is not a coincidence that bullies find themselves in smaller, restricted situations, small closed environments where they can thrive. It is increasingly more difficult for them to operate in the glare of corporate procedure.

But for our example, knowing that you are not alone, that you have allies and support, should reduce your stress and enable you to feel happier. Planning how you are going to deal with this disruptive person will be time well spent. The first step is to diffuse the effects of Doreen's behaviour and the power she exerts over her colleagues.

The best medicine

Let's take the worst thing Doreen does – the public humiliation of colleagues. The next time this happens – and you must be ready – the whole team must all burst out laughing! This will not be so difficult as it sounds. You have planned it, you anticipate the moment. The power that comes from joint action, and the subsequent release of tension, makes laughing very easy. You are waiting for the bully – and Doreen is a bully – in your organisation to start so that you can have fun. That is something bullies hate because they lose their power.

It happens: she is off again, in front of customers, loudly bemoaning her colleague's demands, and everyone laughs at Doreen. "Oh, you are a hoot!" "You love to make a fuss!" "What a character!" "What do you do for an encore?"

Is someone bullying you at work? Could you get a team together to laugh at them? Can you really see them repeating their behaviour? (Be ready to repeat if they do!) What is the worst they can complain of – that you were laughing?

Just running that scene in your head has a delicious quality. How soon can you do it for real on that person in your organisation who is disruptive, who takes pleasure in picking on people one at a time? Instead of everyone keeping their head down, fervently saying to themselves, "Oh God, don't pick on me!" you have a bunch of colleagues secretly wishing, "Bring it on!"

Get organised, take some control and use laughter. And watch the bully wither! I hope this will be successful for you – and that you find yourself laughing all day long. This laughter is not to be cruel but to break the pattern. Not to mock but to change the mood.

You can involve your ineffective boss in this strategy. In fact, they should be involved, as it will help them to grow in confidence in their role.

Now, of course, not all hardened bullies will cower at the first peal of laughter. You do need a consistent strategy – as when dealing with the other mad bosses.

Matching behaviours

Bullies only grow in confidence if they are assured of the compliance and lack of retaliation from their victims. Imagine that – in the same way that you created a wall of protective laughter – you now, as a team, produce a sudden and very aggressive response to the bullying behaviour.

Having worked together to build confidence, to create laughter and mutual support, you are now in a position to do the aggressive response. This will be the inconsistent part of the strategy. You need to be over-the-top and extremely aggressive back to your bully. Time and place is everything – and this may not be possible if you are serving customers, for instance, in the shop. But if you do, give it back to them in spades. What do you think they will do?

Imagine that you could swear really foully and fluently straight back at your bully. Look them in the eye and really mean it. Sure, this is slightly risky behaviour, but how bad does it have to get before you take action? You need to do enough to shock your bully – who until now has had it all their own way. You are not performing alone; get support from your colleagues, and then you can all take part.

Use this technique intermittently, because as with other strategies, overuse dilutes their power. Whom will the colleague-bully complain to? Not the boss, because you have involved your by now grateful, ineffectual boss in this strategy. What can they do about it?

Doing nothing

Maybe the third strategy, changing your response by doing nothing, is going to be more challenging. You won't know until you try it. As in training dogs and children, sometimes the best thing to do is to ignore the bad behaviour. It sounds easy, but takes some nerve. Not only do you simply ignore them, you remove yourself physically. When the bully addresses you, you turn your back on them and walk away.

The golden rule for this strategy is to not react at all. Don't look at them, do not make eyecontact, do not answer or respond in any way whatsoever! This will frustrate the bully. And you will be demonstrating the basic martial art technique of not being there when someone wants to attack you!

For any really bad individual be prepared to use this on a daily basis. Unless part of your job or instructed to do so, do not communicate with the bully for any reason. Avoid them. Laugh within their earshot and act as if they are invisible.

Sadly, bullies themselves have often suffered some terrible trauma that has led them to behave in these ways. However, this book is essentially about how you survive. My primary concern is with *your* happiness at work and dealing with the stress you are feeling. Only when you are sufficiently empowered can you afford to explore their problems.

So where is Jo in all this?

If you have involved Jo in planning and executing the strategies as outlined above you should find she is feeling more confident too. She will have realised that she, in a way, is being bullied as well. She has learned that there are ways to confront people and that you don't just have to be liked. (If you have enough influence, you could perhaps encourage her to start the formal disciplinary process. Most companies have a disciplinary procedure, which involves a number of warning letters, disciplinary meetings, and so on. Find out what they are.) Everyone has seen the mistakes the bully has made and the rules they have broken; now is the time to tell head office and put it into a formal process.

If a boss like Jo cannot find it in herself to control the situation between colleagues then you may find that involving her in a process like the one described above very successful. They will welcome a strategy that helps them to exert authority. Getting them to get to grips with 'leadership' skills may be beyond your capability and is certainly beyond your remit. The main thing is to smooth your workplace and take away any discomfort in your role.

This boss profile will never have had any leadership training and, in fact, the concept will be completely alien. They will have an experience of the boss being the boss and telling them what to do: this is how their own bosses, who have consequently let them down, have treated them. They are like they are because they remember how they hated the bosses they had in the past who were aggressive and dominant, and strive not to be like that themselves.

If left unchecked this type of boss rarely makes it to the next stage. They fail to get promoted to a more senior management role because of their lack of action. If they allow any bully element in their team to flourish they will only be facilitating misery in the workplace.

Fuzzy leadership

The other problem in this scenario is that when Jo was absent the leadership was fuzzy. Teams that operate on a very level playing field can be successful in some companies, where perhaps everyone is of a similar age, education, and experience. But in this situation, where the team was of a mixed background, it would have been much better to have had a very clearly defined process for understanding who was in command when Jo was not around. If you have this situation in your workplace, ask your manager to define the roles and responsibility more clearly, then when the boss is not around the person in charge will have a clear remit that they are in charge and can issue instructions – expecting them to be followed.

In your workplace you may recognise the very friendly boss, who likes to be welcomed and really be one of the crowd. You may find yourself asking them to rectify a situation, which you can see they are reluctant or unable to tackle. Instead of allowing the situation to continue, manipulate a process to help them find a route through the issue. You are acting as a good role model for handling certain forms of aggression, and this will stand you in good stead when you are moving on. Creating allies at all levels in the workplace is undoubtedly a good thing.

Managing a *No Power* boss

Summary:

- Remind your weak boss of their obligations
  - The consequences of failing to ensure safety procedures
  - The danger of non-intervention
- They are friendly so capitalise on this
  - Make suggestions
- Support a young/inexperienced manager – they do have some attractive skills
  - Help them to deal with *their* boss
  - Include them in strategies for changing situations

Chapter Eight
I Hired You, Now I Hate You

Quick check this boss:

- Very easy interview and hiring process
  - ◆ Initially, a friendly boss
- But soon turns:
  - ◆ Aggressive
  - ◆ Remote
  - ◆ Unsupportive
  - ◆ Critical
- Distances themselves from you as your manager as well as physically

Links closely to:

- *Friend Then Foe Then Friend Again*
  (without the 'Friend Again' bit …)

At first glance this profile name seems to be totally irrational. Why should anyone change as suddenly as that? But it actually happens quite frequently. So what set of circumstances could create this profile?

Patricia's story

Patricia, a 39-year-old single mum, told me about her experience working in the outpatients department of a local hospital. Pat had been nursing for about 15 years. She wanted to progress her career and had applied for a role at the same hospital, as a sister – in what she understood would be the department responsible for procedures such as plastic surgery and ENT (ear, nose and throat). Fortunately this story has a good ending – eventually – but it was only achieved through Patricia's hard work and self-control in overcoming the manager, Alison, who was responsible for the situation that arose.

Patricia remembers that the interview with Alison went very well – probably far too well. Alison was the matron who managed the department Patricia hoped to join, and although they didn't know each other very well, had bumped into each other on a few occasions around the hospital.

> *"I really liked Alison straightaway. It was like talking to an old friend, not someone who was interviewing me for a new job. The time ran over, we talked about our kids, our lives, as well as some of the work-related stuff. We just got on so well, she gave me a really big hint that she was planning to offer me the role and I left on cloud nine. I couldn't believe it had been so easy. I had held back from applying for that type of role for literally years, thinking I was not up to it. My kids were now old enough to care for themselves and I felt ready for a new challenge. Now the job I had been hungry to do for years was about to be mine, and with the added bonus of having a great boss like Alison to work for. Alison had a reputation for being one of the best matrons in the hospital; she was well respected and professional. I was looking forward to learning from her, and the challenge of improving my skills.*

> *"Within a week I had the offer letter in my hand, I couldn't wait to start. I will never forget my first day in my new dark blue sister's uniform, I felt so proud of myself and really excited about the new duties and the challenge ahead."*

Everything was looking very good for Patricia, and she was raring to go. Unfortunately, things started to unravel with alarming rapidity. By the end of the first day Patricia was a shadow of the woman she had been at 9 o'clock that morning.

> *"It was absolutely awful, like some terrible nightmare. The job was nothing like I had expected. I felt completely out of my depth and was literally shaking, I was so anxious. None of the procedures were*

familiar to me. I went to pieces. It was obvious the nurses on the ward were getting irritated with me, I was constantly asking them what to do. I know they would not have minded if I had just been asking where things were but I was struggling with things they thought I should know. It seemed to get worse and worse; as that day dragged on I felt my confidence draining away and my memory started to let me down. I was forgetting the simplest instructions and couldn't remember details from one minute to the next. This was totally unacceptable in that environment and I knew it. What had started as one of the happiest days of my work life had turned, in just a few hours, to a nightmare."

How could this have happened? Patricia had been through the interview process, people had been asked about her internally and nothing had alerted anyone about any concerns with Patricia. It had looked like a reasonable and long overdue promotion for a nurse who had excelled during the whole of her career.

Patricia remembers how she finally got through the day and went home, extremely tired and upset, wondering what on earth was she going to do:

"I remember thinking, thank God, I can speak to Alison in the morning and we will work it out. I felt sure she would find some way of getting me up to speed and through this nightmare. As soon as I had started that morning I had realised that the ward was actually focused on general surgery! I had not worked in that area before. My panic during that terrible first day was compounded by the effect that fear creates: you can't think, you don't listen properly and you forget what you have known for years. But anyway, I was really comforted thinking about how I would speak to Alison the next day and resolve the misunderstandings."

The next morning Patricia arrived early. She had not slept very well as she was still so worried about how she would sort things out. She headed straight for Alison's office and was pleased that Alison ushered her straight in and shut the door. However, from that point the meeting did not follow the route that Patricia had anticipated. Even if she could have imagined Alison being cross about the situation (she had received numerous reports about Patricia's poor performance throughout the previous day), she could not have imagined in a million years how aggressive and angry Alison became.

> *"If I had thought the day before had been a nightmare then that meeting took me straight back in! I was crying and she was shouting, 'How dare you mislead me!', 'Why didn't you tell me you were not really up to the job?', 'What on earth had possessed you to apply in the first place?' She was furious; she told me she was completely embarrassed by me."*

This would prove to be the kernel of the problem. By recommending and choosing Patricia for the role Alison had put her professional reputation on the line. She had made a mistake, and was now very angry with herself – but it was going to be Patricia who was going to carry the can.

It had all gone wrong because they had made the mistake of liking each other so much. They had both let the interview process drift from an assessment, as it should have been, to a far less formal structure. They had both, because of so much common ground in their lives and an instant rapport, made assumptions about Patricia's suitability in terms of experience and knowledge. Patricia had not asked enough questions as she was inexperienced in that environment, and Alison had slipped from her normal professional mode. She had followed up on references from Patricia's old department but nothing had alerted her to the disconnect in Patricia's training which meant she would struggle in a department where she had no background experience.

But Alison was stuck in a difficult position, it would be a difficult professional climbdown to fire Patricia, but it was going to be difficult for the ward to accommodate a sister who was supposed to be a leader in the department, knowing less than the nurses working for her. In this particular environment it is necessary for the sister to be ahead of the nurses and be able to direct them. What could she do?

Returning to the ward, Patricia felt completely abandoned. It had been made clear in no uncertain terms that it was up to her to rectify the problem. She would have to 'get up to speed' on her own and that Alison could not give her any 'special' treatment.

Patricia was devastated, but she managed to find enough strength to carry on. Perhaps it would not be so bad – she had learned 'on the job' before, and she really didn't want to fail.

A general ward in a busy NHS hospital is not an easy environment in which to learn. Potentially, an error here can cause a far more serious effect than a mistake in the business world. The nurses in the ward did try to help but were frustrated by Patricia's knowledge gaps. They frequently lost their temper with her. Some tried to avoid being on the same shift, some were openly hostile. Alison took a bit of a back seat in the process, watching, as it turned out, for her opportunity to criticise. She was not at all helpful. Whenever the nurses complained, she would remark, often within Patricia's hearing, that, "She had been recommended."

Patricia made mistakes. Two written warnings were issued and eventually she was demoted back to nurse.

> *"I was punch-drunk," admitted Patricia. "The first warning letter was devastating. That was not the sort of thing that happened to me. I had not written up a drug sheet correctly – it was part of working under such stress – and was accused of failing to maintain 'safe practice'. When the second letter came it was nearly a relief. I had allowed one of the nurses to administer a drug that I should have supervised. It was a minor mistake but again 'following safe practice' was the reason. I knew that this meant I would be demoted and that in some ways the nightmare was over. I can hardly describe to you how awful it was to return to the hospital in my old light blue uniform and face all my old colleagues, feeling like a complete failure. But despite this, I didn't feel as bad as I had been feeling over the previous few nightmare months when I had been struggling with a role I couldn't manage, hostile colleagues and a complete lack of management support or recognition of responsibility."*

Alison had been distant throughout this process. There was no sign of the relationship that had blossomed at the interview. The interview had been the weak link. Each side had failed to stick to the process. But the responsibility should have been with Alison, and once the mistake had been discovered it should have been immediately rectified either with Patricia receiving the training she needed or an agreement secured to release her from the role in a mutually acceptable way. As it was, Alison allowed her pride to get in the way, and Patricia's demise was inevitable.

At this point, she could have pushed for constructive dismissal, but it would have been difficult as she had not actually followed the strict processes correctly. Or she could have appealed to Alison to get her the training and quickly! But unfortunately, Alison had become so unapproachable that this was not an option. Even though it would have saved Alison's face and saved Patricia the heartbreak, this breakdown in communication meant that was not possible.

However, that is not the end of the story. Patricia's behaviour from then on could be construed as her 'going forward' strategy. Patricia was partially responsible for the situation but still had a hunger to fulfil the role and prove herself to Alison and her colleagues.

In this particular case, Patricia went back to her old role and steadfastly worked in her normal reliable and solid way. About eight months later, another sister role became available in the same hospital. Patricia felt that with her confidence rebuilt she would apply again. This time she was much more careful at the interview stage.

> *"I can remember asking so many questions and really checking what was expected of me. I made notes and arranged to contact the matron if I had any further things I needed clarification on. I really did my homework, found out every detail of the role and then crossed my fingers – I was sure I could do it, and I really wanted the chance to prove myself again!"*

There was going to be one problem going ahead, and that was that the matron was going to speak to Alison, as part of the internal reference and checking process. Patricia was terrified that the experience she had had just months before would mean that her reference from Alison would hinder the chance that she would get the job she really wanted.

> *"I decided I had nothing to lose. I had to face Alison and find out what she was going to say. I knew that if she was going to give me a poor reference that would mean I couldn't even hope to get the new*

role. I called into her ward and luckily she agreed to see me. I told her about my fears. I asked her if she would be giving me a poor reference. This was not really like me but it was making me mad, I wanted to prove myself and these feelings were the ones that were driving me. She was again like the person I had met the first time. Now that I had no impact on her ongoing success she had no reason to hold me back. She even sort of apologised. It had really been up to her to lead proceedings at our first interview, and she acknowledged that she had not done that well. She said the way I had gone back to my old role, faced my colleagues, and got through the process had really impressed her. She said she had no concerns about recommending me for the job I wanted. I knew then that if I didn't get the new role, it wasn't because she had stopped me."

Patricia was successful in getting her new job and went on to wear her dark blue uniform again. Her determination in carrying on to get the role she wanted paid off. She did not resort to losing her temper, or losing sight of what she really wanted. She acknowledged her share of the blame in the interview process.

Was her boss mad?

Alison was a professional and experienced manager but she had made a mistake and did not know how she should deal with it. She could have taken control and responsibility and done the right thing by Patricia and her ward.

When I interviewed Patricia, she was loath to criticise Alison, but it was clear she had gone through a very distressing time. At any point it would have been possible for Alison to support her – but she didn't. Alison had options open to her: she could have arranged some training or a quiet change for Patricia to facilitate an early exit from the ward, but she chose not only to turn her back but also to fuel the frustration voiced from the ward's nurses to make Patricia's work life a misery for months.

You may ask why Patricia didn't resign. When I asked her, she told me that she was feeling incredibly insecure, had children to support, and was literally living each day in fear. What would happen to her if she resigned? Where would she go?

Patricia's long-term strategy worked. Eventually she was reinstated with 'full honours' when her new promotion was awarded. She enjoyed the admiration of her determination from her colleagues and friends. Although there were other ways she could have dealt with this situation, her route enabled her to move forward with a sense of achievement. This is another of those events that offers the opportunity for you to become an exceptional manager yourself, especially if some formal training is added to your experience.

Strategy for *I Hired You, Now I Hate You* boss

Patricia showed incredible strength of character in being able to return as a 'failure' to her old team and then return as a success to her new role. Because of the type of person she is, she did not elaborate on how bad things had become during her time in the general surgery ward. Can you imagine being practically paralysed with fear and in a fog of ignorance and going in day after day to face unhelpful colleagues and an unsupportive boss – and with no sign of help on the way? She was constantly treading on eggshells around all those other nurses, forever watching for the next tiny mistake. In such a position, she was embarrassed to call herself a sister.

In this scenario, the situation arose from the breakdown in communication resulting from Alison's pride and Patricia's fear. Patricia did have other options open to her, but it is unlikely that these would have produced a better result. For example:

■ Patricia could have talked to Alison's boss. There would have been an opportunity for her to voice her unhappiness and share what was happening with a more senior person. But that would have probably soured her relationship with Alison, because Alison would see her promotion chances dwindling.

■ She could have tried to re-engage with Alison to try to find a way for them to agree that a mistake had been made. Then they could have decided upon a joint strategy, as basically they still had respect for each other.

■ She could have spoken to old friends and colleagues who would have reassured her that it was not such a terrible problem after all. They could have reminded her of her successes and good times. I cannot put too much stress on how important it is to check in with old friends and colleagues whom you trust to 'sanity check' your performance.

It's often the case that companies, departments and, no doubt, hospital wards become so institutionalised, so wrapped up in their procedures, that they forget that new people need time and help to get up to speed. Patricia's problem was compounded by her fear. With her confidence eroded, she was unsure of herself and not clear how to rectify the situation in which she'd found herself.

■ Putting your head above the parapet to check out your employment options is also an option, but when in this state of mind you are unlikely to have a positive outcome from a distracting and draining interview process, as well as trying to cope with your role.

In essence, the strategy is: Stick at it. If you were hired, then you were right in many ways, if not all. If there has been a disconnect in the communication of the role, address it very aggressively as soon as possible. Facing your fear head-on is a great way to dissolve it. Patricia faced her fear when she went to ask Alison if she intended giving a poor reference for the new opportunity. It was a shame she could not have approached Alison in this way before. I can assure you that in such situations, do not expect the boss to apologise at any stage; for them, that would be seen as a confession of culpability.

If the situation gets really bad, be very careful. You do not want to permanently damage your confidence or health. If at all possible, take a short break to regroup, and apply to the private healthcare sector and earn twice as much ... Seriously, if at all possible, take a short break. It's the best way to enable you to take a step back and decide your strategy. Even a couple of days off with a 'sickie' can give you the chance to unwind, see the situation for what it is, and plan a way forward.

Managing an *I Hired You, Now I Hate You* boss

Summary:

- Talk to the person who hired you as soon as possible
  - ◆ Don't compound the issues by trying to cope
  - ◆ You don't want to put others at risk
  - ◆ Are you partly to blame?
  - ◆ Did you suspect there would be some trouble coping with this new role?
- Focus on why you wanted the role and use that determination to fulfil it efficiently
  - ◆ Do you need a training course, a mentor?
- Take a quick break
  - ◆ Work out the best route to recover the situation
- Talk to ex-colleagues
- Remember the skills you have

Chapter Nine
Sales Manager

Of all the mad bad bosses, there is one who is badder and certainly madder than them all ... the sales manager.

'In the end, somebody has to sell something ...'

Anon, extract from CV

Quick check this boss:

■ Inconsistent
  ◆ Aggressive, followed or preceded by:
  ◆ Delightful
  ◆ Mistrusting
■ Lack of 'big picture' vision

This boss links closely to

■ *Mr Long Hours*
■ *Friend Then Foe Then Friend Again*
■ *Fear Merchant*

Sales manager is the role that can manifest all the clinical symptoms of bi polar disorder – but you won't need the confirmation of a qualified psychiatrist. These folk make the *Friend Then Foe Then Friend Again* boss look like a well-balanced individual. They make the *Power Crazy* boss look like your best friend. It's time to delve into the mad world of sales ...

The truth about what happens in sales

Yes, this is what is probably happening today in your organisation. Read it and weep.

There is an amazing charade acted out on a regular basis – Monday morning, or Thursday afternoon, every week or every fortnight – across the country, across the world, where thousands play out the farce that is the sales meeting. The sales team will typically be a small group of employees who are cajoled, often abused and almost always pushed into making that fine declaration known universally throughout the sales world as the 'sales pipeline' or 'sales forecast'. They speak a special language, and engage in a ritual which to outsiders appears strange, even nonsensical. However, for the participants, this event is the time their total agony is manifested as they come face-to-face with the maddest boss of all.

This meeting is led by the sales manager. The longevity of a sales manager within an organisation rarely exceeds one year, because their success is invariably rewarded by having their target doubled. Unable to face the strain of tackling another year of pressure chasing a totally unattainable number they pack up their lists of contacts and leave. Most sales people within an organisation outlast the sales manager who allegedly controls them because the level of expectation resting on their shoulders is less. The sales team may find they are allowed more than a season to deliver because they are 'building pipeline', or have a 'good forecast', but the sales manager knows the greatest stress of all and that makes him completely mad. Employers are then just able to ride the small wave of success the manager has created – but that crest can all too quickly subside. Sales managers are thus somewhat mobile, and changing to a new role from time to time at least enables them to hold on to their sanity.

Increasing the target is more magical thinking than realistic forecasting. In the heady environment of an end of year board meeting, these mad bosses allow their greed to run wild. Given the success the sales manager achieved, their dreams of doubling the size of the company in the next 12 months can now surely be realised. This is the common insanity of many a venture-backed or start-up company ... greedy to cash in on their new venture as they plan to 'share' it with the world ...

To deal with the fantasy, the sales managers will either move on before their failure to reach the 'number' is evidenced, or reach the number and then have it doubled! They move from one organisation to another in a state of perpetual aspiration. Each new employer welcomes them, believing the amazing tales of 'business growth' and 'lead generation', and embracing the hope that these newly acquired sales skills will cure all and satisfy the financial hunger of the organisation. Blind eyes are turned to the previous miserable failings of this strategy; extreme optimism is the order of the day.

Every sales manager carries a backpack of best ever success stories, and find they are always able to blag their way into pastures new. They paint a picture of 'huge pipeline', of multiple, influential contacts. These are the messages that the new bosses want to hear, the messages they want so very much! They are only too willing to believe these stories of success, because they need sales! They crave the sales saviour, and he cometh – with the new shirt, exquisite cuff links, expensive shiny shoes, and old-but-classy immaculate car ... The hopes of the company are pinned securely to the new manager's bulging Rolodex. It doesn't take a genius to work out that this is madness. And you are working for him!

The new sales manager arrives full of confidence (sales managers must by definition be full of confidence and optimistic – I am sure the gene for 'sales manager' will be identified soon) because the new employers have told him it's the right market and that the company has a product with a bucket full of USPs (unique selling points). But this confidence is not to last. Once in post, the new manager, wooed by these tales, discovers that the situation is not quite as rosy as the company bosses painted it. Maybe these people simply deserve each other ...

Sir Lunchalot

Within this maddest boss of all profile, there are a couple of subsections. There are those who believe that there is a direct correlation between the number of times you take a prospect to lunch and the number of deals you close. This profile I fondly call Sir Lunchalot. He will make you feel wonderful and could seem like your best mate. But if he can blame you for the poor sales results you will be fired in an instant. He's the sort of manager who can deliver the following type of communications:

"Well done, we have increased your target."

"Well done, we are firing you."

"Well done, we have discovered the sales mix is wrong and the company is not making any money."

"Well done, I'm afraid the main investor is pulling out, so we are letting the sales team go."

and yet you will not feel angry with him because he expresses it in such a way that it doesn't feel like he is blaming you, nor that this was his decision. It won't seem too bad, as this guy never burns bridges. You will be picked up and then dropped from a great height. He will be the sort of boss who offers to 'smooth things over' for you when things are going wrong; sales are not happening or not happening quickly enough.

Sir Lunchalot will regale you with stories of what happened twenty years ago with 'old Jonesy' who is now a director for the company. This guy is a terminal sales person; he will be doing it till he dies. He has beautiful manners but drinks like a fish. He 'should have been promoted' to a much more senior position some years ago, but no, he just couldn't cut it. His addiction to expensive ties and his total lack of ability to see the business from anything other than his point of view has precluded any promotion.

He is mad, but in a way that makes you laugh and cry all at once.

The obsessed sales manager

Another sales manager profile is the type that only lives to deliver targets. All else in his life takes second place. He is just as self-centred as Sir Lunchalot, but a lot more scary. He will have had the blood in his veins transfused with company branded blood. He will act as if his very life depended on the success of the sales team. He will micro-manage you, he will look like a hunted animal, having forgone sleep to design a spreadsheet, a PowerPoint presentation, or a reporting tool. He will question you if your expenses are too high, and if they are too low!

He is the person suggesting satellite tracking be installed in company cars. He refuses to accept any word you say as truth because he has burned through so many lying sales people and cannot conceive of you being any different. He drinks too much coffee and thinks herbal tea is for wimps. He is not as polished as Sir Lunchalot, but they share the same ingrained traits. You will be there only so long as you make them look good. They are only impressed by one thing: How much have you sold? And they don't care how you do it.

In other words, forget any kind of review process that incorporates objectives, training, team-building or any other company window dressing on the topic of investing in people. Sell – or you are out. To put it mildly, this scenario will require you to have some specialist protection and survival strategy.

Selling is one of the most rewarding careers. It is rarely dull, and it gives you amazing highs to compensate for the deepest lows. However, should you wish to keep your sanity when surrounded by madness, you need to cultivate a calm view over the proceedings and be able to rise above the mayhem. Keeping your head and seeing things in perspective will directly affect your success, because by not allowing yourself be distracted by the frenetic activity of your mad boss, you will be able to focus on those practical sales activities which will reward you.

By recognising the traits of the mad sales bosses you can prevent them from damaging your confidence and your performance. Unless you manage your mad bosses, their anxiety and stress will negatively affect all areas of your life.

Both profiles see the end of the sales/financial year as a cut-off point; if you are in the unhappy position of being under target, you may be highlighted for replacement. They will be completely ruthless. Your dismissal may be more or less tactful in its execution, but always remember: they don't really like you, they never really did, they are completely selfish, and if you can't contribute to their success then you are out. As with the end of any relationship, they will rewrite your story in order to have something to tell the new sales person who will replace you.

Careful …

When you start your new sales role ask what happened to your predecessor – and listen carefully. What are you hearing? Have they made changes to their processes, pricing or product range that will mean your success is more likely? If no part of the process has changed, can you really expect to be successful if your predecessor was not?

In my experience, if you are replacing a previously dismissed sales person (as opposed to joining a team), proceed with caution. What seems to have been the reason your predecessor failed? Was it the company, the offering, or the sales manager? Probe deeply in order to extract the details of what really happened; this will be extremely useful information. Don't assume the employer is telling you the truth, especially if the answer contains comments such as, "He was not a good closer" or "She was a slow learner." That's a glib way of blaming the sales person. However, if they tell you the guy was fired for running a high-class lingerie business in parallel to selling software, believe me, that may be true …

You have joined a company with a great product range, so why should you not succeed? Sure, there are competitors in the market, but you are good at your job. Hang on a bit: check out the products you are going to be selling. Could they possibly be of poor quality, obsolete, or over-priced? What is their visibility in the market? What is the business world or the stock market saying about the company's reputation? Is it renowned for its cock-ups? No, no surely not …

I am sure that the delivery of your product is perfect, that your fulfilment department always delivers on time, with the right size, colour and quantity, and the product always works perfectly straightaway. Implementations run smoothly? Yes, of course … And your customers are always delighted with the billing and invoicing process, the simplicity of its presentation, its accuracy and timeliness, with your friendly credit control team. Great … lovely … marvellous!

No? I thought so …!

What goes wrong?

Too many organisations focus too closely on the sales team. When things are going wrong they tend to carry a disproportionate amount of the blame on their shoulders. Sales teams suffer more churn than most other parts of an organisation. If you really had all the factors above sorted, would you fail? Without these factors in place, what chance do you have of succeeding? In such a company, your first task will be to understand these issues before you can perform your role as sales person.

Typically, the company is caught in a repeating cycle (Figure 9.1). It gives me some wry amusement to notice that however many times they go through it, so few organisations learn.

	1. Company has operational/product/reputation issues.
	2. Company under pressure to radically increase sales.
	3. Company hires new sales manager. (Big, big expectations ...)
	4. Sales manager hires new sales team.
	5. Company trains new team in products, market and process.
	6. Team fails to make target because of operational issues as above.
	7. Company fires the trained team for failure to meet target despite investment in time, training and effort.
	8. Company still has not addressed the operational/product/reputation issues.
	9. Company still under pressure to increase sales.

Hiring a sales manager cycle

Repeat *ad nauseam*. And don't mention the cost! As long as the operational and other issues persist, the company will be severely challenged in trying to meet its targets, whether it hires the very best sales people or the worst.

This scenario, perpetuated by short-sighted senior management who fail to recognise and address wider company issues, gives rise to the maddest boss of all and for all the misery and stress about to be experienced by the hapless players in the sales team.

The story that gets promulgated internally is: "Don't worry; it will all be OK because the shiny new sales manager, backed by his greatest and latest team will make all those issues go away." As if by magic, just by hiring this marvellous new team (yes, you), all the product, operational, marketing and brand issues evaporate ... Hurrah! Let's go spend the commission!

Many large organisations feel no guilt at gilding the lily somewhat in order to entice a big hitter into their organisation. The incoming manager really wants this new opportunity (remember where he is coming from). Having made a limited investigation into the company's background, his eyes glassy from the size of the basic salary offered, he's only too willing to accept the position. The company, equally culpable, want the saviour to ensure their success and ignore the fact that the guy has had 5 roles in six years. The scene is set; let the mayhem begin!

Robert's story

Robert worked for a local paper selling advertising space. Although in this sector there are not many local papers to compete with, you are fighting for what is often the meagre advertising spend of small local companies or sole proprietors. Helping them create campaigns that will bring tangible benefit is the challenge. They will have only a limited amount to spend on advertising – and other media are fighting for their share of it.

Robert had worked in other sales jobs but he was excited about starting his new role at the Herald. Andy, the Herald's young sales manager, welcomed him. Robert begins his story:

"Andy, the sales manager, made it all sound so exciting at the interview. He could barely sit still. He painted such a great picture. I was to get a company car, I would be out and about all day. He had great plans to drive the success of the advertising in the paper. It was only after I joined that I found out he had only been in the job for a month himself and had already ousted my predecessor. Andy had come from a local free ad paper and thought he knew everything about the business. I found out that, because of his previous success, the Herald's owners had given him practically free rein to make changes. He had money to spend and aggressive targets to pursue. The owners knew that in order to survive the Herald must compete against not only the free papers but web advertising, trade magazines, and other campaigns in which local businesses may have decided to invest their advertising budget.

"I thought, this is it – he is so motivated, we will be heroes! I couldn't wait to start and work with Andy. I was going to make tons of money and be a real success. It all felt fresh and new. The Herald was a high-profile local paper and the name itself, I felt sure, would make it easy to open doors."

Robert started work. The environment that he encountered was charged with the infectious energy of Andy. Andy had set high expectations for his management team, and was feeling pressure from them to deliver results. He had spent their money, fired the incumbent team and was promising results … And now Robert was in the team.

Robert's excitement was not to last.

"I can remember Andy at the first meeting of our new team; there were two other guys and me. Selling display advertising space for a local paper is not rocket science but there are certain rules and processes to follow that help your success. I had been hired for my sales skills, but was still fairly new to advertising sales. Andy quickly got frustrated when I asked questions about some of the topics. He made me feel that I couldn't ask him stuff. I realised his energy and sense of excitement also meant he was impatient and short-tempered. He told us what he was expecting in terms of revenue – advertising space

bookings over the next fortnight. I didn't know if they were unrealistic or not. I was new to the industry so innocently didn't comment. I was still feeling good about my new opportunity and confident I could make an impact."

Robert remembers spending the next couple of weeks on visits to businesses around the area. He made numerous appointments, helped put together advertising deals and quotes for countless companies. He worked really hard, he worked late. He would liaise with colleagues back in the office who would help him price out work and advise on options and timescales. He felt good about the work he was doing and spoke to Andy every couple of days. He felt everything was going well and did not have any concerns about the sales meeting that was due two weeks after the first team kick-off meeting.

"God! That crazy meeting! Andy was like a man possessed! He had a face like thunder and seemed to be almost shaking with emotion. He was so angry and I really didn't know what I had done wrong. He told me my figures were terrible, that I was utterly clueless, and that he hadn't hired me to sit and drink coffee all day in customers' offices. I tried to protest but he just wouldn't have it. He did eventually calm down a bit. He was equally aggressive to my colleagues. He said he needed to know what business I was going to bring in over the next two weeks. I told him I had been getting to know my territory, the business people in the area and that I was sure that the relationships I had been building, the quotes that I had been creating, would bring me the business he expected. I gave Andy my list of prospects, but far from keeping him calm it seemed to get him mad again. He then went through a process which I have now heard friends in sales tell me about. He asked me to pad out the list to include people with whom I had only really had an introductory phone call."

It's worth mentioning this is more detail because it is the pain of the sales meeting. If you are new, young, junior or nervous in your sales role, you must fight this from the beginning. Your sales manager wants to prove to his bosses that he is being successful and will 'bring in the bacon', justify his big salary and his big spend on you! If you present him with your realistic sales pipeline, and it's anything less than double your target figures, he will go through your activity for the previous period and scrape together a huge list of deals that are based on nothing more than a hunch or enquiry. In other words, he will pressure you to create a pipeline that although completely unrealistic will satisfy his mad bosses.

Is this a joke, or is this a joke?

Why is this so laughable? Because there will come a time in the not too distant future when this fantasy pipeline will come back to haunt you.

As you progress through the sales cycle the scene changes according to the time of the year, the quarter or the month.

Back to the weekly sales meeting. It starts with the sales manager asking each sales person to report on their activity over the last week or fortnight: Who have they seen? Who is a prospect? What is the probability of closing such and such piece of business …?

Now, of course, this would all be fine if everyone colluded at that meeting and agreed that, whilst the pipeline looks good, it is unrealistic and should only placate the bosses until the team delivered the real business. It would be fine if you could be sure that your mad sales manager understood that the pipeline was a work of fiction. But by the next meeting they will deny that they ever forced you, they will forget the haranguing, the challenge they set you of producing the pipeline they demanded. They will forget that they asked you to forecast deals, which you implicitly told them amounted to no more than a hunch and a handshake.

I know about this story. It's my story. I can't deny it. I have seen the mad sales managers cry and beg, the ones that demand and scream, those that abuse and ridicule. They are the mad sales managers!

The sales manager reviews your excellent work, notes you are on target, and then goes into dramatic mode. The office door is shut behind you and there you are, face-to-face with a nightmare.

Well, not exactly face-to-face: your boss is sitting on the desk, putting you in the low status position sitting on the chair. From on high, your mad boss sets about you: "You can do better!" "If you really put your mind to it, you could be well above these figures!" "You are so lazy – when I was in your role I delivered twice as much!" They shout, they slam their hands on the desk and generally attack you, as if that is going to make you work harder, be more loyal or deliver a penny more of business ...

This kind behaviour is even directed at the most successful members of the sales team. Why? Because the sales manager has had to work so very hard for his success. It's another example of "I had to work so hard for my success, so if this person seems to succeed so easily, it makes a mockery of the effort I had to put in." Essentially, they resent any easily won success.

In the face of this madness you declare your 'sales forecast' – which includes fictional opportunities from every person you have spoken to over the last week, any contact, any business, your mother, your sister, the man who served you at the garage ...

Robert experienced the full works when he returned to the next sales meeting two weeks later. With a boss as mad as Andy he could, of course, not expect any support for the padded pipeline which they had colluded to create, and which Andy now needed to be real and delivered.

Robert continues, smiling, as in retrospect this appears ludicrous. But at the time ...

"Andy was looking like thunder again, but I was not so bothered about that. I thought I knew what was coming. I had closed nearly 80% of my 'real' target so he really couldn't be disappointed in that, could he? But he tore me apart! He shouted at me 'your pipeline is a fantasy! What are you thinking putting all these deals on the list when you have so little information!' I started to blurt out 'but, but' until I realised that it was hopeless. He had pushed me two weeks ago to tell him about everyone I had had any contact with. Huh. I learned the hard way. I made a very bold internal note not to be pushed again. I started to see how he was operating, pushing everyone really hard, hardly ever being pleased, and always wanting more. It was not an environment for the faint-hearted."

Sales protection

One thing sales people are often accused of is 'sandbagging' – a technique used to protect themselves from scenes such as the one above. If you have been abused by a sales manager for 'creating' a list of deals you may decide in future to be more 'discreet', shall we say? You may know about a piece of business that's on the horizon, but you are a damned if you are going to tell anyone about it. The moment a sales person refers to any opportunity with a pulse, the manager and the manager's boss jump on it like it's a hot prospect. It appears on their radar and you have the constant questions, enquiries and pushing to get updates. Sometimes the best tactic is to keep quiet and tell them only when you are ready. That's not ideal, but it is a way of getting some peace. Then you deliver your great deal as a surprise. In the same way that you may be tempted to take a 'sickie' when the stress gets too bad, this strategy too has to be used with caution. Again, you need to build in an element of being unpredictable. If you always sandbag, they'll expect a sandbagged deal, even when there isn't one.

Robert soon saw that Andy would just push, push, push the team to deliver in order to satisfy the targets he had set out for his bosses. Robert's challenge was to find a way of not reacting to him in a way that would detract from his own success. One solution was to take the time necessary for building relationships with the local business people – trust does take time to build. Robert knew he was doing all the right things and that he was on track to meet all his targets. The last thing he should do at this stage should be to jeopardize the relationships he was building and become unprofessional in his dealings with the local business people.

People like Robert have sales in their genes. For them, sales is a wonderful world, it's the only world. You're selling all the time. You sell to your kids, you sell to your partner and you sell to strangers in the street. Should you ever find yourself in a role that doesn't need you to sell, no matter, you'll find something to sell anyway.

The downside is that this is a world that fluctuates wildly, and brings with it huge amounts of stress and pressure as well as great satisfaction. At times it will all get too much and you'll feel like just walking away. Even though he loved being a sales person, Robert was approaching that stage.

The profile of the sales person

Sales people can be a sad bunch of misfits, aspiring to large salaries but more often than not lacking the necessary education to fulfil this desire. In exchange for the eye-watering rewards they might achieve they are willing to accept the roller coaster of emotional highs and lows. They may sometimes come across as somewhat shallow, insincere, or materialistic – but most of the time they have to be. They get abuse, pressure and constant rejection. Unlike their non-sales colleagues they have precise targets that cannot be avoided or fudged. They are expected to deliver and the spotlight is on them. The obverse of this reveals a much simpler being who seeks recognition, who loves to be rewarded, not just in monetary terms, but for the glory of making 'club' or being the 'top'. When the sales team delivers, the whole company breathes a sigh of relief. Their motto really is 'Sales is King', and they get the excitement of being part of the entourage.

Team player, or not?

Do sales people need to be team players? There are two schools of thought: either be a loner, score the goals, make the deals and to hell with everyone else; or be a part of an environment where the sales team is urged to bond to help and support each other in what is a challenging task.

This latter option, as you can imagine, generates conflict. In most organisations you do not get fired if your colleague doesn't make target, which kind of negates the notion that this group of people operate as a 'team'. More likely, sales people are judged according to their personal results. What possible benefit could a sales person derive by helping a colleague, spending time with them, showing them the ropes?

Despite this, my advice is that you should be a 'team player' – however, with everyone but your fellow sales people. With them, you remain courteous and friendly. The people you need on your team are the delivery people, the support network that looks after your customers – and you. If you are going to beat your sales colleagues, you need to ensure everyone is well-motivated to process your orders, implement your systems, pay your commission, and yes, really, go the extra mile for you! Look after these people! Remember that this is almost certainly the background of your sales manager.

GSOH

Another key characteristic of the winning sales person – 'team' player or a bit of a loner – is that they need to have a great sense of humour. Although this might contribute to the misconception that sales people are shallow, the ability to laugh – at oneself and at life in general – is a necessary part of the preservation instinct that allows you to survive constant rejection, and recover from frequent rebuttals.

Robert had a clear idea of how he wanted his sales career to progress and he was not ready to be pushed out by a mad boss like Andy. Therefore he decided that he was not going to leave the job, but would somehow find a way to change how Andy was making him feel. He understood that Andy needed to make him successful, which is why he had been chosen. Robert was going to make great salesman and it would be a negative and costly process to have to replace him. Andy had a boss to whom he had to justify his actions.

However, Andy's behaviour was completely mad, his meetings were wild and always included table thumping, swearing and criticism of the sacred 'pipeline'. When Andy was really under pressure he could on occasion resort to begging, screaming or crying. If you have experienced melodramas like this, it may help to realise that you are not necessarily the problem – any number of other factors may have triggered the outburst. For example, he may have just discovered that a competitor has launched a product at half the price, knowing that his own manufacturing/delivery/fulfilment operation is behind with production. He is more than likely remembering the mad promises he made to his mad bosses and be very worried about how he is going to report on performance to them.

When a new manager accepts a sales role, there is probably a conversation with the new employer which includes the following comments. After a period with the company Andy would be in a position to see the truth behind those comments:

"We have barely any serious competition in the market."
"Well, actually we do have competition, and as most of our products were designed 15 years ago, we are out of touch."

"We have an exhaustive (exhausted?) customer base."
"This product line is in fact pretty niche and we will need to invest in some serious R&D to make sure we continue to hold our position with the customers we have."

"We have a professional and motivated team for you."
"They are fed up because their expenses haven't been paid; they are keen, but some are new and completely untrained."

All these issues add to his pressure and, of course, he may also have a hangover …

The sales team become the whipping boys for the operational issues in the company, and the focus of the frustration of the sales manager, who always wants results bigger and quicker than can be delivered.

Sales managers often drive their teams into a sandbagging cycle. The resulting fear and aggression inevitably produces a serious decline in motivation (which is an absolute requirement for every self respecting sales person). Soon the sales manager's head will be full of:

"I don't trust sales people."

"He will be off as soon as he has closed that deal."

"Sales people never mean what they say."

"The sales team are a load of jokers."

The reason why he thinks like this because he was one of 'them' before his promotion to manager. He thinks he knows just how their minds work. Now, as the manager, Andy may have no one to discuss his issues with; he is alone with his pressure. What will happen to him if he fails?

Robert's strategy

Robert found a strategy to cope. The sales meetings at the Herald continued on much the same lines. Sometimes it was Robert in the line of fire, but Robert became used to Andy's animated histrionics and refused to let that undermine his confidence. The more aggressive and angry Andy became, the more Robert found he was able to be calm, to step mentally away from the situation. Because if you want to stay sane and successful when working with a mad sales manager, you do need time out to reflect on what's happening. He ignored the bad behaviour, just as you would the tantrums of a child. He absolutely would not react to it. The key was staying rigidly consistent in the face of pressure and stress.

Robert knew that if he became distracted by Andy's behaviour then his work would suffer. He maintained the 'hygiene' factors – he was always smart, on time and was always where he said he would be – therefore giving Andy no reason not to trust him. He positioned himself as conservative, careful, and considered. He constantly replayed the truth as he wanted them to hear it. He irritatingly always understated his future business. He would ask colleagues to back him up. ("You know we are unlikely to get the order this week. You know Mr X is always slow …") He refused to be squeezed on his pipeline forecast, repeating mantra-like the numbers he wanted to put forward.

Such a strategy means you have to be in peak form day in, day out if you are to cope with the extreme pressure of a demanding sales role. Eat well, avoid junk food, not too much alcohol, get plenty of sleep, and exercise (at least to work off your frustrations). Pay attention to your nutrition and fitness. Suffice to say, if you abuse your body and burn the candle at both ends you will not do your best in the uncompromising world of sales. You will get emotional, miss out on opportunities and let yourself down.

Steadfast consistency

Robert had faith in himself and knew how he should treat customers and prospects. He was building trust and a good level of business by being consistent with them. Clients and prospects need to trust you.

Beware: some organisations put so much pressure on their sales people that they begin to behave in ways that are unpleasant and in some cases unethical. Don't let this happen to you! You know what's reasonable, so stick to it. Be true to what you know is right – or you'll find yourself featured on an undercover TV show. Do not hassle your prospects with a barrage of phone calls or visits. Do not contact them continually to try to put together the 'right deal'. Communicate with them appropriately. Any inappropriate communication not only damages your relationships with your customers and prospects, it will also damage your career, and your opportunities for doing business with them, and anyone they know, in future.

Trust

Imagine that you dealt in a courteous and professional way with everyone you made contact with, from receptionists to CEOs. What would be the result? A network of contacts who will only ever speak highly of you and your behaviour, and tell other people about you.

Sir Lunchalot, mentioned earlier, is an expert at this technique. That is why, even if he has to fire you, he will do it beautifully. Learn from him, he is a master of the power of the network. Don't burn bridges, you never know when today's junior executive will be tomorrow's influential decision maker. People you are talking to move company and role, and you may only have a small chance to make a good impression on them.

By behaving in this way you will ensure a secure career, not only by delivering sales, but also by doing so in a professional and ethical way. Don't let anyone else ruin it for you; they will probably not be around for long.

Dealing with Andy

The techniques described in *Friend Then Foe Then Friend Again* around behaviour will be useful. You need to keep yourself a little aloof and distant from a boss like Andy, who is likely to turn on you in unexpected circumstances. If he changes his story on pricing, products or any essential information you will find the nuts-and-bolts strategy (see pages 53-54) useful: record all the details of meetings and calls. This is good practice anyway, and it's pretty easy to do.

Being unexpectedly aggressive back to this type of boss can also be effective. They can get used to just shouting at everyone, but what would happen if the whole team simply walked out. He needs his team, would be severely criticised by his bosses if he lost you. I'm not suggesting you use this risky strategy, but it's nice to know that in extreme circumstances you could …

Remember that whatever pressure you are feeling, your boss is 'getting it' from above too.

His bosses hired him as the saviour and expectations are running high. The sales team can make him look like a hero or a zero. Andy has been hired – but not trained (which would certainly help). He would also benefit from some humour being injected into his life. Many successful sales managers try to develop very close personal relationships with their teams – so that the team feels loyal, doesn't want to let their manager down – or possibly lose him and have a nightmare as a replacement. Clearly, Andy would have benefited from some loyalty from his team, but he would have needed to earn it. He needed some fun in his workplace.

Team-building

You can still influence the mood of a sales team even on your own. If you decide to risk getting closer to your mad sales manager, especially if he has had little or no training, introduce him to motivational activities. Show him how he will benefit from having your support and loyalty. (See, for example, some of the ideas in the Fun Stuff chapter.)

If he won't open up to team-building, exclude him. Make arrangements to meet with other sales people (probably outside work hours) and let him know what an effective meeting it was. You might just have a couple of pints down at the local, but he doesn't know that. He will want to be a part of things; force him to realise he must be.

If things get really bad, and with this madness and pressure it can happen fairly easily, have a day to yourself to think about your strategy. Don't be fired or pushed out of your job. Make sure you are in control and make the move you want. Sales people often wait for a commission or a deal to come in before making their move, so time it well. If you really can't see a future within the current operation, use this time well to find the best next move for you.

Patterns of behaviour

Before you take on a sales role, check out 'what usually happens' within the company. What happened to your predecessor? What are the chances of your success? What is your new sales manager like?

I used to believe that of all job roles, the people who became sales people were 'coin operated'. That they would put up with any sort of environment, just so long as they were paid enough. I know now from experience this is not true. Sometimes the pressure from sales can be so great that sales people will walk away from a large commission payment or deal because of the misery they are experiencing. Like everyone else, they need to be treated reasonably, but in reality, they are often abused.

Whatever your level of frustration, it is never a good idea to lose your temper with your manager, it's never the best strategy to walk out. Keep all your options open, do nothing you will regret. By following the strategies explained here you will increase your chances of a successful sales career, and a reasonable working environment.

Managing a mad sales manager

Summary:

- Distance yourself, be aloof
  - ◆ Don't let their hysterical behaviour get to you
  - ◆ Recognise it from day one
- Be consistent
- Build trust
  - ◆ With customers
  - ◆ With your manager
- Learn behaviours to counter their inconsistency
- You are building your career, don't behave in a way that will damage it
- You know the right way to behave – do it!

This boss links closely to:

- *Friend Then Foe Then Friend Again*
- *I Hired You, Now I Hate You*
- *Mr Long Hours*

Chapter Ten
Fear Merchant

Quick check on this boss:

- Stern
- Charming, but cool
- Aggressive communicator
- Encourages cliques
- Manipulative
- Unpredictable

Institutionalised Fear Merchant – Companies that culturally embrace fear as a tool

Typically:

- High risk/high reward roles
- High staff turnover
- Aggressive training/targets
- 'Fast tracked' management opportunities

This boss links closely to:

- *Friend Then Foe Then Friend Again*
- *Small Business Owner*

What's different?

You may be wondering how the *Fear Merchant* differs from the *Power Crazy* boss. Here's what distinguishes them.

The *Power Crazy* boss implements company process in his usual frenzied manner. He toes the company line and enjoys pointing out where you are not delivering according to such-and-such rule. He closely examines your work at all times, but he does not necessarily have his eye on a bigger goal; he's focusing on you.

The *Fear Merchant* is a different animal. He won't care about how you work, but he will be very interested in what you deliver or achieve.

There are two variations of the *Fear Merchant* boss. But the outcome is the same: they generate misery across the working world.

One type of *Fear Merchant* is the individual who controls his own little empire, which is full of frightened subjects. He may be the business owner, or someone working within a much larger organisation.

The other sort of *Fear Merchant* lurks within organisations that culturally use fear as a 'management tool'. Fear is encouraged by the organisation. Managers control and drive their employees with it, and deliberately hire unsuspecting individuals who are vulnerable to this style of management. Finding yourself working for either is still bad luck; they can be hard to spot at the interview.

Organisations that culturally instil fear have fine-tuned the relevant techniques and are specialists in using these methods of management. They regularly use the 'negative interview' process. They have badges and names for different teams, groups, levels. They create tables and leagues, scores, targets and conversely 'shame lists', 'losers' and other negative versions of the groupings.

The Fear Merchant – as an individual boss

The *Fear Merchant* in a small organisation, or where they are the business owner, has a clearly observable sphere of influence; but within a large organisation, such people carve a niche for themselves and create a micro-world which they control through manipulation. They are able to manipulate some surprisingly strong characters. They weave their fear to make sure of securing their own success with a range of objectives: their next job, meeting a target, delivering a service or product, a promotion ... Whatever they are driving for they ensure that the context in which they are working will guarantee success in achieving their aim.

They often appear charmingly self-assured, and use this as part of their strategy to control you. At the heart of their manipulation is the way they manage their relationships with their staff. I have encountered at least two different scenarios, both where the manipulation is based on fear of being 'out' rather than 'in'.

The *Fear Merchant* is surrounded by a clique of favourites. If you are not part of this 'in-group', they create situations where you become desperate to be 'in'. How does the *Fear Merchant* do that? Because everyone aspires to be a favourite, it takes very little to get people to collude and to ridicule those who are 'out'.

The favourites get a nickname. This nickname may not be entirely politically correct, but of course that's OK because it's a nickname, it's given with affection, and of course he's not really racist or sexist, is he? He will push to get away with the most risqué name possible. It's part of the control. The reality is that outside of the *Fear Merchant*'s world such nicknames are derogatory, but the subjects put up with the name because it gives them more chance of being 'in'. And surely this name has been given by the boss, who is in control, so it cannot be meant negatively, can it?

So 'Fatty' (I don't feel the need to submit more examples) will be our chosen example.

> *"Hey Fatty, can you get us a coffee, mate?"*

> *"Hey Fatty! You're the Man, you OK to drive me to the airport?"*

> *"Hey Fatty, you are so fat! Man, he eats all day, he never does any work!"*

> *"Gee Fatty, I think I'm gonna have to let you go if you get any fatter, man!"*

"Hey Fatty, good job on the work yesterday, did you need to eat extra?"
... and so on.

It's 'harmless fun', isn't it? He is the butt of jokes, he knows the boss can take it further and further. He lets him. Does it start to undermine him? I think it does. It gets out of control. Imagine a whole team where the boss is slowly undermining staff through veiled, intermittent discrimination. Sometimes you are the butt of the joke or criticism and all your colleagues are laughing at you. Why? Because these others are only too relieved not to be the target themselves.

If you are willing to challenge these behaviours, there can be a happy outcome, you can learn from this kind of boss. There is also a dark downside. If, over time, you allow this type of boss to erode your confidence, this may easily spill over into your personal life. His constant put-downs and control of your career can cause serious damage.

This boss's influence can also expand across time and companies. I have seen grown men who, due to a misplaced sense of loyalty, follow bosses who treat them in this way from one role to the next, two, three or even four times. The boss cites it as a favour: "Come and join me, it will be like the old days, the old team, together again!" – but is in fact taking his little gang with him, to make him feel good, just like the bully gang-leader. It may look like loyalty, but it's also the cost of being a favourite of a charming boss who can manipulate a team. His friendliness is fake.

Others working for this type of boss have found themselves at the doctor's surgery. When confidence gets really low, it not only affects your working life, but can result in serious depression.

This sort of boss will suppress your career as well as your confidence. This may impact you financially and will certainly restrict your promotion opportunities. If you don't have confidence to confront this sort of boss or resist his games – stay away!

Aggressive language

On its own, the nicknaming may not seem a major issue but it is accompanied by other behaviours. Our *Fear Merchant* boss communicates in highly aggressive language. It is intended to threaten; it is normally over the top, and does not allow for any discussion on a decision.

An email telling you about a meeting will include words such as 'mandatory', 'compulsory' and 'absolute', like this ...

> To All Operations Team
> Jenny
> Kick Off Meeting with C.W. Ltd
> This meeting is mandatory. Anyone not able to attend the meeting should report to me immediately with a comprehensive explanation. No casual wear will be permitted.
> Any persons failing to represent the company in line with the Stated Rules will be punished.
> Absolutely NO excuse for lateness will be accepted and will result in an automatic warning letter.
> JW

The style is typified by:

- No greeting

- Sign-off – initials only

- Every line is a threat

- Highly aggressive

- No option for refusal/non-attendance

The *Fear Merchant* boss strides into the office/factory floor/showroom with a very stern face. This is another part of his style. He looks very serious, deep in thought, unapproachable. He gives the impression of being important, of carrying a great and serious burden, the responsibility for which he alone carries. He regularly fails to be even averagely courteous: no "Good morning" or "How are you today?" He may nod to a favourite. He's being clever; he is the boss!

Another way to create the aura of importance is in how you react to things. In an open plan office/environment the *Fear Merchant* boss does not just open a letter or email and quietly note the contents. No, he immediately curses. It's dramatic and it attracts the attention of the people around him. But he never says what the communication contains. He will do this regularly; sometimes he'll slam his hand on the desk as well.

The *Fear Merchant* boss is fond of 'one-to-one' meetings, especially with his boss. After all, they have so many very *important* things to discuss. If you have a meeting with him he will tell you that he has many serious things to worry about, but hey, he's managed to find five minutes for you.

This boss is part actor, part prima donna, and building his path to achieve *his* objective. Through manipulation he gets people to do extraordinary things, show amazing loyalty, and go to great lengths to please him. They don't want to incur his wrath; they are reminded of his temper on a daily basis and they don't want to be on the receiving end of his aggressive communications. They can see from his face that he is preoccupied with very serious issues. They want to be 'in', addressed by their nickname, but not to amuse colleagues. Heaven is to do something for him in order to be praised, not ridiculed.

It all works fine – until you fall out of favour and are ousted from the group. Thereafter you are doomed to be a victim, the subject of amusement, abused and rejected.

How on earth do you cope with this?

The very style of this bully means that it is unlikely that you can enlist the support of colleagues. However, recognise this boss and you will almost certainly enjoy the spectacle. He won't be constantly on your back nagging you about your work so at least you can get on and do your job. There are ways to communicate with him that will work for you, and may even disarm him. Mirror his communication style: be brief, be aggressive, and forget the niceties. Always look him straight in the eye when speaking to him. He may have the habit of invading your personal space, which in the office environment might mean that he takes a position where he can look down at you – both literally and metaphorically. If you are sitting at your desk and he perches on it, stand up, but keep close to the centre of your territory, so that you take control of the 'space'. You don't want him feeling he is getting the upper hand.

The toughest thing to follow through on is not responding should he address you by any name other than your real name. Just don't answer, turn away, ignore his attempts to bait you. It's tough, but do it. Eventually he will give up. You will be making the decision to exclude yourself from his game. He is not stupid; once he realises that you are not going to succumb the chances are that you could end up with a fairly good communication channel with him. So long as you don't damage him, restrict him or cause him any trouble, he will leave you alone.

In reality, he is a classic bully, and if you confront him, he will fold like a pack of cards. If you are not confident about this then don't do it. However, on every occasion when I have confronted this sort of boss they have become completely placid, rolling over like a puppy. They don't want trouble, they normally have their own agenda, for which the job is the vehicle. They just don't care that much about you and certainly won't risk upsetting their apple-cart if you have a genuine gripe.

Some of the strategies described in *Friend Then Foe Then Friend Again* may get you a little distance and help you regain control by not allowing him to take you, your behaviour or your responses, for granted.

How to manage the *Fear Merchant* boss

Summary:

- Don't play the game
  - ◆ Don't react to his body language ('I'm important')
  - ◆ Don't let him call you anything but your name
- Confront him
  - ◆ Start small
- He doesn't deserve your loyalty!

Other ways to motivate

Motivation/manipulation

The *Fear Merchant* boss and the fear culture try to control and manipulate by bullying, scaring and humiliating you. Motivation is the technique used by smarter organisations. These two stories offer examples of good and bad practice of how companies can use tactics to motivate/manipulate employees. The differences are clear, and are good examples of each.

A company had around 15 sales people in its team. Each of them had a company car. Suffice to say, all bar one was from a major German car manufacturer. The odd one out was a non-aspirational car previously manufactured by an Eastern European company, oh, OK it was a Skoda.

Each month the lowest performing sales person had to take the non-aspirational motor vehicle. This created a competitive but light-hearted atmosphere. There was always, of course, a lot of high-spirited banter at the sales meeting when the results were announced and the car allocated for the month. Knowing as we do the motivators of the typical sales person, this was a powerful way to drive them to achieve. This was a fun way to encourage their sales people to do well.

At the other end of the scale, a mini case study from an IT support professional, in his own words, and it's to do with how a company manipulated the allocation and use of company mobile phones.

"We were given company mobile phones for when we were out of the office. We were told that we could use them for limited personal use and that anything above a limit (£30 for me) would be deducted from my salary. Fine, I thought, so I used it, not excessively, but knowing they would ask for a contribution if I was too excessive.

Anyway, about six months later, we get hauled into an office one at a time and given a dressing down about using our phones too much. Some people who were office based had their phones taken away. We tried to explain that we thought we had an arrangement but were told we had abused the system.

Next thing, we are being told we can use them for limited personal calls as long as we were contactable 24/7. A requirement to be permanently on call for no extra money, we thought. We were asked to sign a letter saying this was OK. Some of us (including myself) gave the phones back and said 'no thanks' and were labelled as 'the trouble-makers'."

Isn't that a great example of hot mad boss action? The technique of one-to-one meetings to 'persuade' each person that they had made a mistake about the arrangement, and then their change to allow the phones but in exchange for free 24/7 support availability is classic.

I understand that organisations need to use methods to encourage people to do what they want, but as you can see from these two examples, there are some really excellent ways to do this and some really poor ones ...

Working in the Fear culture

Summary:

Quick check this boss/culture

■ Recognise the scenario you are letting yourself in for

■ Don't expect this role to last forever

■ Take all the training on offer

■ Good for your CV

■ Not the place for the overly sensitive

This boss links closely with:
- Small Business Owner
- Mr Long Hours

Companies which promote a culture of fear

Here's what you must know about an organisation which promotes the *Fear Merchant* culture. You need to recognise it for what it is – bullying. You may decide to join this organisation anyway, but your peace of mind and the success that it will allow you to achieve could rest on you fully understanding what you have let yourself in for.

What education and experience do you have? What level of earnings do you expect? There exist companies who are able to offer – to a certain sector of people – a level of earnings that they would be unlikely to be able to achieve in any other environment. Primarily, these are sales driven organisations such as media sales, insurance, recruitment companies, telecoms equipment, double glazing, and some retail enterprises where the level of remuneration may be significantly higher than for the average job, because they carry a higher degree of pressure and stress – deliberately created by the management.

The reward is great, and the people are driven hard to get these rewards. This is fine if you understand the game being played. Here's how to recognise the game, how to cope, and how not to let it destroy you.

These organisations push and push people by driving and pressuring them. If they succeed, they are rewarded very highly. It's a league-table culture: everyone is ranked according to how much they deliver for the company. At regular intervals, the bottom or poorest performers are savagely (and irrationally) culled. It is assumed that top performers are at the top solely because of their individual performance. Random fluctuations, and the effects of the system they are in, are ignored. Top performers can be heroes one month, but live in fear of dismissal the next, because there are no guarantees over the short term that they won't suddenly be at the bottom of the list because of naturally occurring market changes. Anything less than annual performance analysis does not work to a top performer's advantage if you are only as good as your last result.

The other tools that generate pressure are targets, deadlines, arbitrary timings, standardised training, bonuses, rewards against demotion, humiliation, and threats of dismissal.

Continually striving for the highest results can burn people out. They can become as aggressive as the employer who is rewarding them. It is a cycle of not only financial reward but of recognition. The company hails the victors, cites their aggression and tenacity as highly desirable and worthy traits. It's tempting to mimic these behaviours, but often it is at the risk of your own sanity.

Rarely do top achieving sales people maintain their position year after year because the pace and the pressure are so high. You have probably met examples of this. If you accept that you are joining such a company because of greed – you want that big fat pay cheque – then that is fine, so long as you know what else to expect.

Jack's story

Our next case study is from Jack, who lives in California. His story is that of a typical 'second jobber'. For two years, after leaving school he had worked as an office administrator, realising too late that it would have been a better option to have extended his education when he'd had the chance. He would have given himself far more opportunities in relation to employment. Alas, he felt he had missed his chance to do anything about that. He became interested in advertisements placed by a national jewellery chain looking for sales people in their retail outlets. The adverts also talked about the 'speedy' career opportunities for the 'right people', with the chance to become a manager in a fairly short time. The money offered seemed too good to be true. He applied.

The interview

Jack's first experience of the company was the negative interview. This is a technique to test how you react under pressing circumstances. If you are unaware of the purpose of this interview, it can be distressing. The interviewer sets out different impossible scenarios for you; for each you must describe how you would resolve the problem. The scenarios become progressively more extreme. They increase in severity, and eventually you give up being able to offer solutions and leave the interview feeling terrible, a failure. In my experience, this turned into confusion when a short time later the person who had interviewed me phoned to say that I had got the job. I didn't realise what had happened.

Jack remembers his interview:

"It started off OK, I think … The guy was very smart, but I remember thinking he was wearing way too much jewellery – but I guess that made sense! He asked a little about my background, about what I wanted to achieve. I told him I wanted to make lots of money! So then he starts describing a problem that might happen at one of their shops, like a customer complains that a necklace has broken, it is faulty and we need to replace it. Then we find there isn't one in stock, what should I do? I say to the guy I should call another shop and get it shipped over for her to collect. Then he says, well what if she complains again because it's a present for her niece at her wedding and that's tomorrow. So I said I would arrange to have it collected from the other shop and sent out to her. Then the guy says what if they then find they don't have another necklace exactly the same, not even in another shop. So I say we try to repair the original one. Then he tells me the guy who mends the jewellery is off sick, what do we do now?"

"It goes on and on like this till you cannot come up with anything constructive. At the beginning it seemed kind of fun and challenging, but that only sucked me into to game, so that by the end, I was feeling bad because I felt for the poor customer, because I couldn't solve the problem! I didn't spot the trick the guy was pulling, so I thought he must think I'm real dumb".

"The interview ended, he shook my hand, and said I'd got the job! I nearly fell over, I was that surprised. I couldn't believe how that happened."

Jack only found out weeks later after he had started work that this was the standard technique. The companies who use this say it means they can be sure that someone won't get too aggressive in a difficult situation, for example, which might possibly involve a customer. On the other hand, it is a flawed process, as the interviewer can't know if the interviewee knows the technique, and is just playing along. They may still end up with an employee who has the potential to punch a customer.

Jack started work at the jewellery store. It was big shop and most of the time very busy. A major part of the remuneration was based on commission, so it paid to 'hit' customers as soon as they walked in the door to find out what they were looking for.

Jack continued:

"We found that people generally came to the store already intending to spend some money. They may have seen something they liked in the window, or wanted a present for someone special. Our job was to make sure they spent as much as possible, more than they had intended. The company had around 30 stores across the country and we were all ranked on sales reports that were published every week. Each store had around eight to twelve sales people and we were all ranked as well. You could get bonuses for being top in store, top in state, top in region, and top in the country. Yeah, the 'top' guys could make pretty good money. Everyone wanted to be top! That was the key. For everyone else it was pretty tough. The top sales person in the store would get the pick of the customers, for example, if the store was empty and someone walked in, he would get to approach them. The company believed that if he was top then he would have the best chance to make a good sale. Everything was geared to help the top guys; everyone else aspired to be one of them. We could all see it was possible to make the big money, and we all worked like crazy to get there, but it was hard if you didn't get a few breaks."

Jack explained further:

"The guys with the poorest sales each week used to get a really hard time, at the after-work sales meeting. Once figures were read out and

we knew who the weakest guy was, the manager used to lead the chant, "LOSER! LOSER! LOSER!" Man, no one wanted to be that guy! If you were the lowest performer for a month then you got fired! That was also pretty mean. The managers would march the guy straight off the premises on a Friday night. It was meant to be like public humiliation – he was made to feel like a real failure. Gee, I saw so many guys come and go, some of them took it really bad. But the worst of all was if you had been top. I managed to get there after about eight months. I worked very hard, never took a break for lunch, coffee or holiday, I wanted that big pay! Course the company knew no one could keep up that rate of work, that's why they always had the other guys ready biting at your heels …

"You are top for a while, you get the big pay, but you know there are loads of guys waiting to take it off you. The manager reminds you everyday about that! You become so aggressive – your manager encourages that, he wants you to work your guts out. When I lost top position, I lost more than just the money. Being top gave me some sweet perks, like discount on goods, extra holidays, but worst of all you lost the respect. The manager went from calling me 'The Man', all high fives and backslapping, to shaking his head when he looked at me, sometimes mouthing the word 'loser' at me across the shop floor. That drove me nuts!"

Jack followed a classic path with the jewellery store. He realised what the score was fairly early on. He achieved top spot but realised he couldn't maintain the pace. When the sarcasm and humiliation started he just took it as he had seen so many other guys go through it too. He left shortly after losing his top spot and managed to miss his 'loser' walk of shame.

"When I realised exactly how they operated I felt like I just took a step back and saw it for what it was, and that kinda helped me cope. Some of the other guys went crazy. There were days when I felt like thumping my manager. They didn't care one bit for anyone that worked for them; we were like battery chickens. If you weren't top you hardly earned any money, it was always just chasing that top spot and always someone ready behind you to take it. I was burned out at the end, I

couldn't sleep and everyday felt sick at the thought of having to go to work; I hated those guys."

I hope this illustrates how these organisations create a fear-driven environment.

But you may well be wondering: Is it a false economy? Although driving high sales, these organisations lose out in the following ways.

- Continuous hiring and firing – cost implication
- Getting a reputation as a poor employer
- Pressured staff – do they make the best sales people?
  - ◆ No one likes the hard sell
- Tense environment in the shop
  - ◆ Not an enjoyable shopping experience
- Disgruntled ex-employees
- Given a more forgiving pace, these sales people could have produced for considerably longer
- Losing valuable skills and knowledge

The managers of the stores are encouraged to make employees scared of the consequences of not delivering, to highlight failure and to use public humiliation, sarcasm, and aggression to drive this fear. You may say that the employees deserve all they get – they are just greedy for the reward. Well, that may be partly true, but the role and its proposition is rarely explained in advance. It can be a bit of shock when you have previously worked for 'normal' companies and don't realise what you have let yourself in for.

Additionally, these companies target the most vulnerable candidates. The manager will rub his hands in glee when he knows he has interviews with a young dad with a new family to support, or a single mother trying to cope with childcare and provide for all the other demands her position dictates. The more you have on your plate, the more welcome you will be, because they know that once they have you, you will be desperate to keep the job, and you will WORK! These days, the more debt and responsibility you have, the more attractive you become to many employers. They know you will not fail to get up in the morning, and they are going to take every advantage of that. An organisation with this type of institutionalised fear is in a good position to exploit this vulnerability.

The coping strategy

The main way you will cope is by recognising and accepting the job for what it is. Some individuals will always be exceptionally successful in these scenarios, but remember how many people the company will have churned through in relation to this small number of 'successes'. If you can rise to a manager or head office position before you lose your sanity, then good luck. For the bulk of the workforce it will not be the longest tenured position.

Play the game; yes, throw yourself into it. If you know it's a play-hard work-hard environment, don't try to study at the same time, don't do it when you have other complicated things in your life to juggle.

Learn from the top performers – ask them how they did it, get as much information as you can. If you can get to be one of the best, it is something to have on your résumé forever.

Remember the managers are directed to use the fear tactics described here, so don't take it personally. The more subtle behavioural techniques described in the *Friend Then Foe Then Friend Again* boss will most likely be lost on this crowd. But don't lose yourself. This environment rewards aggression, but try not to take it outside of work. This is harder said than done. You don't have to be 'top' in your social life; ask for honest feedback from a friend if you think you may be losing it!

Look after yourself. Don't burn the candle at both ends if you expect to get in top position. Watch for signs that you are burning out. I developed a very distinguishing twitch in one eye when working for one company that practised these techniques!

Managing the *Fear Merchant*

Summary:

- Be realistic about what you are getting in to
    - ◆ Don't take things personally
- See everything in its right perspective
    - ◆ Don't expect it to last forever
- Don't take the techniques home
- Enjoy the glory of being 'top'
- Look after yourself
    - ◆ Live healthily – you will need your energy
- If it does start to get to you, have a sickie and remember these points!
- Attend all the training courses, they can go on your résumé
- Don't ever accept that this the norm, it's a style for these companies

This culture links closely to

- *Sales Manager*
- *I Hired You, Now I Hate You*

Chapter Eleven
Small Business Owner

Quick check this boss:

▧ Cliquey

◆ Can be especially so if a family business

▧ Intense

◆ Few people to dissipate emotion, problems, triumphs

▧ Lacking trust

◆ They have to hand their 'baby' to you

▧ Petty

◆ Because of the trust issues they want to know everything that's going on

This boss links closely to

▧ *Power Crazy*

▧ *Mr Long Hours*

▧ *I Hired You, Now I Hate You*

The Small Business Owner boss

I have known some great business owners who have the vision and the leadership qualities that you often find lacking in much larger, high-profile organisations. But things can go wrong. For example, the boss has been in charge for too long and has lost touch with the outside world. They can become bogged down, trying to do too much of the work themselves because they do not fully trust their employees. They may be under pressure to cut costs; they get exhausted trying to cope with so many different responsibilities. The small business is their livelihood, this is their baby. When they have to hire staff, they feel they are releasing a little of the business, but they really don't want to. It takes a special type of small-business owner to regularly look outside his organisation for inspiration, new ideas, and new technologies.

Another source of trouble that can arise in more established small businesses is that they become insular, and this has some potential dangers. This can also happen within a family, or to any specialised team or department within a large organisation They create their own little world, and develop behaviours that within the group go unnoticed because it has become the norm, but to the newcomer or outsider it seems bizarre, unacceptable or even offensive. Employees can find they are stuck with bosses who behave like tyrants or dictators, out of step with the world beyond the confines of their particular shop floor, production unit, distribution centre, and so on.

How do you manage if you find yourself in this situation or are already suffering in this environment?

Working for a Small Business Owner

You may find yourself working for the aspiring entrepreneur who has set up the business. Now, it is very difficult to start your own business. You launch, daring to hope that all your dreams will come true and that in a few short years you will be rich and no longer required by the business on a day-to-day basis. You, of course, will be sunning yourself on a golden beach, sipping cocktails.

Unfortunately, the reality can be quite different. Having already worked a long day, the small business owner has to spend cold winter evenings poring over the accounts documents – which just does not match their early glamorous dreams. Then, on top of all that, they cannot do it all themselves; they have to employ other people, who, unfortunately, may not share their vision, and probably do not have the same level of emotional investment in making the business succeed. What's more, these employees have every right, protection and insurance in the business, and for which the owner has the privilege of paying!

Could I have painted a darker picture? This owner boss profile can be a recipe for disaster. They want to run a business, they have to have people, but the fears they carry can create a miserable workplace. Over time, they can become jaded, even if the business is successful. Experiences where employees let them down can damage their already distrusting nature and this may manifest in the poor treatment of subsequent new recruits.

The strategy for this scenario is slightly different from previous examples. It is based on the belief that unless you are intending and able to marry the boss's son or daughter (or even the boss himself), you are highly unlikely to have the sort of success in terms of career development you might expect from a large corporation.

The main thrust of this strategy of coping with a business owner is theft! Of course, I am not talking about the removal of physical goods, intellectual property or anything of any quantifiable value ... I am not advocating criminal acts, so perhaps I should call it 'education'?

Paul's story

"It wasn't difficult to get the job. It suited me. I lived locally and was interested in clothing and fashion. It was a neat and stylish shop – I could remember going in there with my Dad when I was little kid to buy his suits for the office. I knew I didn't want to work in an office so after a stint in a big supermarket, thought it would be a good move to go to an independent retailer. I had heard he was considering opening additional shops and I was keen to learn the trade. The shop was so smart it felt good just to be there. The interview was brief and seemed uncomplicated. He explained what he expected me to do, the hours, the pay: that was about it. I remember being so pleased! I didn't really ask any questions at all. I just let it all happen to me. The boss asked me why I wanted the job and was satisfied when I told him about my interest in clothes. He thought my retail experience in the supermarket would make me a good trainee in their shop."

Paul found himself working in his home town for a small business, an independent men's outfitters. He would be working alongside two other sales assistants and the owner, their boss, whom we shall call Andrew.

What could he have asked during the interview process? What could he have found out about his prospects? Could he have spotted any warning signs about the possible behaviour of a boss who was also the business owner?

The main thing he could establish during the interview was the likelihood he could progress to become a manager himself. Naturally, at this point, regardless of Paul's desire to know, it was not feasible for him to ask the boss,

> *"Does being the owner mean you have complete lack of trust and intend keeping as much control as possible?"*

Nor inquire,

> *"As you haven't had any training, do your management skills mean my work-world will be a nightmare?"*

Consequently, Paul could not have envisaged what was to follow.

This experience sadly left him no choice but to leave (as in Stacey's story in chapter four), less than a year after joining. Even so, there are some strategies he could have used. As a rule, the fewer people in a business, the fewer the strategies available to you, so when joining a small company – take care! On the other hand, it may suit you to work for a small company because you prefer that kind of close-knit environment. But that does not excuse poor management. Remember that when it comes to causing problems, the size of the organisation does not matter. It only takes one person. So should you be thinking of turning your back on the large corporate type of company, don't imagine that intrigue, jealousy, gossip or politics stop at the door of a small independent business.

The first thing to become absolutely clear was that Andrew did not share any of his decision-making with his staff. In addition, he was very critical of everyone's work. He knew he had to tell people what to do, but just wasn't good at it; because he lacked trust in his employees, he managed to make every instruction sound like a threat.

Paul continued to tell me his story and was upset at the memory.

"Andrew hated having to rely on his staff. He seemed to be out of his depth, not sure of how to talk to us. After only a few days in the job I was pretty upset. He treated everyone terribly, he was a tyrant! I can remember him coming to the shop, after a meeting somewhere, and making nasty personal comments to everyone. Sometimes when he was stressed about something – a late delivery, or a problem with a particular garment – he would start swearing and being so insulting. We were all supposed to laugh it off, but you can't do that for too long. I remember he never seemed to care if he upset people. I think in some ways I got the worst of it. He saw how it made me feel and I just didn't know how to handle it. The worst thing for me was when I told my parents (and remember, they had been going in there for years), they just couldn't believe it. They thought I must be being oversensitive. If it hadn't been for them pressuring me, I would have left much sooner. Some days I used to pray that he would be out of the shop on a meeting as I just couldn't bear being near him. I think half the time he thought he was being funny, but it was always at someone's expense.

"He would get us to do stupid pointless repetitive tasks. Clean where it was already spotless, refold shelves full of garments, and all the time criticising our performance and making personal comments. It may not sound much, but it was really wearing. I did learn a bit about the business and I enjoyed helping the customers, but there were often long periods when the shop was not busy and then the horrible behaviour of Andrew would continue. All I wanted to do was get on with my job, I was getting more and more miserable. I was really too young to know what to do about it."

More about small businesses

It is rare to see problems like this in a large company, but they do occur. Abusive swearing and petty personal comments will not usually survive under the glare of a corporate HR policy, but as we have already seen, some bosses are able create similar work problems whatever the environment.

In a small business the owner is the Boss. He is also chief buyer, marketing department, the payroll department, HR and the complaints manager. The owner can define all the 'policies' and act without let or hindrance. If you decide that these infringe on their legal requirement for acceptable behaviour in the workplace, you can follow the path of bringing the behaviour to light and try to prosecute them.

Even though there are now numerous laws to protect employees from abuse, it still happens. If you decide to follow the legal path – and that is a difficult decision to take – remember you are making a stand for all employees. It is not easy, but it is a brave thing to do, no less so because it is within a small family business. In a small community, the impact of being known as the person who took a local business to court may be unpleasant, but it may be the right thing to do. Paul decided that he would leave because he was not prepared to go down that route.

Paul was really in shock from the experience, having discovered that even in that small local environment it was possible for a tyrant of a boss to create an atmosphere where terrible behaviour went almost completely unquestioned.

The Story of Mr Christmas

There is an odd phenomenon that I have encountered. Let me tell you the story of Mr Christmas.

How does it happen that such extremes of behaviour are allowed to develop in a closed community consisting of a small number of people? The following story has always stuck in my mind as an example of how really strange behaviour, created by a little clique, can become 'normal', and yet is incomprehensible to outsiders.

An ex-boyfriend of mine told me about a girl he had met who had asked him to spend Christmas with her at her family home. On arriving at the house he was introduced to the family cat, who was usually called Tigger, but whom over the Christmas holiday period was always to be referred to as Mr Christmas! The cat was dressed in bright red bow. A tradition had evolved that every time anyone in the house passed the cat they needed to bow and say, "Good Day, Mr Christmas!" No one in the family could tell him how this quaint little family tradition had started, but they all did it, did not question it, nor think it at all strange. To my friend, an outsider, it seemed madness.

This is a perfect example of the scenario I want to bring to your attention. Within families or within small communities, such as a group of people in a shop, department, or office, behaviours that seem strange or unacceptable in the outside world become normal and accepted. Sometimes you get drawn into this because you want to conform – you're simply matching the prevailing culture. It may seem natural, or harmless, but sometimes the people within the group cannot see that it is odd, and anyway, it is not done to question or comment upon it.

Signs of mismanagement

In a family business – a kind of small semi-isolated community – where the boss can be a petty dictator within his own world, such unthinking behaviour can produce terrible results. Personal comments or abuse go unchecked, and there are examples of how this manifests as poor management procedure:

- Being paid late or incorrectly

- Not provided with the correct equipment for the job

- Unacceptable facilities
  - Unhygienic wash rooms
  - Overheated, non-air-conditioned premises
  - Cold, unheated premises
  - Overcrowded workplace

- Dangerous practices

- Lack of safety helmets and other safety equipment

- No protection from hazards

- Not sticking to safety practices

And that's only the beginning! Little by little, in almost imperceptible steps, the behaviour within one of these communities – with the compliance of its members – slides into unacceptable levels. A newcomer may have a rude awakening finding themselves immersed in this 'dysfunctional' culture, which has arisen partly through poor management, and an unwillingness of anyone in the group to blow the whistle. If you find yourself in a situation like this, and it feels wrong – then it probably is wrong.

It is very easy to get sucked into thinking everything is OK. Check your perceptions with someone outside of this little community. If they can distinguish that your concerns are real, consider what courses are open to you to get things changed – from having a quiet word with the boss, to taking legal proceedings if they are breaking the law. If you feel a situation is genuinely dangerous then leave. This could be tricky with the family business as you are likely to be surrounded by colleagues who find nothing wrong or odd in what happens. However, you don't have to bow and say, "Good Day, Mr Christmas".

Remember that should you take a stand in this type of environment, and complain to a more formal authority, you may not maintain a situation for yourself but you will have helped the cause of those coming after you.

The strategies

You need to adopt a different strategy if you are working for a small or family business. A large organisation offers many more opportunities for advancement – if that is what you are after – simply because of its size. A small business cannot offer so many options.

Assuming that you are going to stay put in the small business, one strategy is to treat this time as an opportunity to learn as much as you can about how to run a business. Your workplace becomes your learning zone, where you can get very close to all aspects of running the business. You could then take this education on to a new employer or use it to start your own enterprise.

In this workplace Paul could learn about:

- Pricing effectively

- Ordering processes

- Window display

- Stock management

- Contacts within the best suppliers

- Sales/marketing techniques

- Basic accounting/bookkeeping

- Advertising/promotion

If you are in an unhappy situation and plan to leave, then learn as much as you can. When you do leave, stay if possible in a similar role because the information and knowledge that you have gathered can be packed away in your portfolio of skills and carried on to the next opportunity where you will be paid a dividend for your knowledge. Do not necessarily abandon a particular industry or type of role completely - all bosses and workplaces are different. Find yourself a better role where your experience will be valued. If you constantly cross into new areas you are not building anything, and thus starting each new role at the bottom with an 'empty basket'. If you really want to change, migrate. Do not leap. The more you build on your experience, the greater the value you can offer to prospective employers. Apart form learning everything you can about the business you will also be learning how not to manage and motivate people.

Although Paul found working for a petty tyrant intolerable, by using this strategy it would have brought him some reward. I am not going to explore the option of marrying the boss's daughter. That, possibly, would have been the only other way forward in the family business – but that too will have interesting consequences in due course.

I would not recommend that your strategy include the behaviour changes suggested for the *Friend Then Foe Then Friend Again* boss. The small business boss craves you to be consistent, reliable and most of all wants to trust you. To build that trust you have to be consistent and not give him any cause for concern.

OK, OK, boss ...!

Now I guess that if you run a really good, first-class small business you will be fuming by now. I know not all businesses are the same, I know you might be doing a great job, and I also know that some employees leave a lot to be desired. Take this as a formal recognition of your excellent work and just ask yourself if there is anything else you could do to help other small businesses see the benefits of treating staff in a reasonable manner? Do you have a sphere of influence in your local business community?

Building your career

Let's imagine that your small business boss is not too bad, he still has a few trust issues and can be a bit intense, but all in all, he's not making your life hell. Assuming you are interested in progressing, how can you fix your career options?

A classic way to build your career in this context is to get a 'piece of the action'. If you have been working for the same person for a length of time – months or many years, depending on the type of business, how fast it's growing, how successful it is and the significance of your input – ask the boss for a stake in the business – ask for a share in the equity.

If you are having an impact on the success of the business, he will seriously consider your request. If you discover he doesn't value your input it may make for a slightly difficult situation. Initially you ask in a very soft way.

> *"Andrew, have you ever thought about taking on a business partner?"*

(You may not be after a partnership – that would cost money – but it will indicate his attitude to sharing his business.)

Having established he would consider sharing the ownership, proceed. His options are:

▪ Keep a really good worker (you) inside and benefiting the business

▪ Lose you, either to the competition, or because you set up your own operation and become the competition

If he allows you to earn equity, perhaps in the form of an annual share bonus/award, it does to some extent solve some of the trust issues. You are now both directly benefiting from the success of the business, you form a better relationship, and your emotional investment should ensure that you, like him, have the very best interests of the business at heart. This is a completely different dynamic to the boss/employee state. It speeds the maturity of the relationships in the business. Clear agreement should be defined and documented concerning the rights and benefits agreed between you when a portion of the equity becomes yours. Get professional input.

Over time, instead of remaining as the employee, you have an opportunity to have a stake in a business that you will have had the satisfaction of helping to grow. Nice!

How to manage the *Small Business Owner*

Summary:

- ▓ Try and understand as much about the culture at the interview process
  - ◆ Ask to speak to your potential colleagues alone
- ▓ When you start work:
  - ◆ If it seems wrong, it probably is wrong
  - ◆ Trust your judgment
- ▓ Decide a plan of action
  - ◆ Legal route
  - ◆ Leaving route
- ▓ Learn as much as you can
  - ◆ The information, the experience are as valuable as the wages
  - ◆ Could you set up a similar business?
- ▓ Try to understand the reasons behind the boss's behaviour
  - ◆ If possible, don't take it personally
  - ◆ Build trust, it's a key concern
  - ◆ If things work out, ask for a share in the business

This boss links closely to:

- ▓ *I Hired You, Now I Hate You*
- ▓ *Fear Merchant*

Chapter Twelve

Boss In Love

Romance in the workplace

Marrying the boss's son or daughter can be a viable strategy for advancement, but that's only one aspect of improving workplace relationships. But before I get into exploring how relationships can affect your workplace, I'd just like to say a big, big thank you to all people I've worked with who were having affairs at work. All moral and emotional issues aside, it's better, more amusing even, than having your own soap opera! The aim for an illicit affair between colleagues is normally to keep it secret. However, it's true that 'love is blind', because for some reason the people involved don't seem to realise just how obvious their behaviour is. I am so grateful for the entertainment it has provided for my ex-colleagues and me over so many years. Again, thank you for the sweet distraction!

Relationships are often a major topic for workplace gossip. It's fun to spot lovers' meetings – during the lunch break, arranging innocently to be on business trips or work/social events together. It's hilarious to watch them stagger their return times after breaks. Yes, for observant staff, watching this couple's antics can be a fascinating diversion – but that is the lighter side. What do you do if your boss has their eye on you? What if they are having an affair and try to get you involved, using you as an alibi, to cover their activity? This is the other darker, less amusing side of office affairs which, in some cases, have caused a great deal of distress to the employees caught up in the romance.

This chapter is about how to cope with the unwanted, amorous advances of the *Boss In Love*, and what to do if your boss attempts to use their position over you to help them pursue their affair.

Watch out! Boss In Love …

I read some time ago of the teachings of a particular management guru who suggested that bosses should love their employees and, just as importantly, should tell them. This is *not* the same. This is about bosses who are attracted to you and use, to a greater or lesser extent, their position to manipulate the situation.

Of course, you will recognise when your boss is 'making a play' for you, but in case you are in any doubt, here are some telltale signs.

He:

▪ Asks for more to 'one-to-one' meetings with you than with anyone else.

▪ Asks you personal questions, that are just a little too personal: "Are you happy with John/Dave/Matt?" (your spouse or partner).

▪ Arranges trips, conferences, meetings, social events that involve time away from the workplace, and if possible with an overnight stay.

▪ Asks you to lunch to discuss that 'possible promotion'.

▪ Finds he is dropping by the place you work/sit/operate more and more frequently.

▪ Accidentally, during discussions, calls you by his wife's or girlfriend's name.

If you haven't picked up on these clues, then you will definitely get the message when you find him waiting outside by your car with a bunch of roses, declaring his undying love for you!

Of course, you may welcome such attention. But if you need or want to keep your job, then the best advice is to steer clear of getting involved. It can be flattering to have the person in charge showing you interest, but it can also damage your career. So before you reciprocate, take a cool look at what you could be getting yourself into. For a start: Is he married? Do you actually like him, or would you rather chew off your own arm? The thing to bear in mind is that even if he is single and an Adonis, what will happen if the relationship ends badly?

Remember the same gossip that entertains the rest of the staff can be very cruel to the lead players in this drama. If there is any suspicion that you are exploiting the boss's interest to obtain promotion, a pay rise or other perks, your popularity will plummet, and the moment the boss leaves or the affair ends, you may find yourself out in the cold ...

The challenge is to manage these advances without alienating the boss, without causing potentially damaging gossip, and avoiding injuring your career path or job security. Essentially the strategy is to say no, and mean it, and avoid hurting anyone's feelings.

Here are some ways to dilute the attention:

- Invent a wonderful loving partner, even if you don't have one. (If you already have a useless one, make them sound wonderful.) Mention them, appropriately, at every opportunity.

- Whenever possible, avoid situations where you are alone with the boss.

- Say no to some requests, especially travel arrangements made at short notice, that seem contrived.

- Avoid working after hours, or meeting out of hours unless you're with other people.

- Don't smile too much – be friendly but not too appeasing or keen.

- Never agree to a hug, not even a 'corporate hug'.

- Never offer any encouragement whatsoever!

It may take some time to finally convince the *Boss In Love* you are not interested. If you want to stay in your job, you'll need to handle such situations with a degree of sensitivity. There is little point in going for a big show down scene – unless you want to get the office Oscar for your performance!

If you feel threatened by any approaches, or feel that the advances represent harassment, then do seek outside help. If you think you have made it clear that the attention is unwanted and yet they still persist, you should seek advice and assistance.[4]

Why it happens

Why do bosses sometimes engage in this inappropriate behaviour? For the same reason that any inter-colleague relationship can develop into an affair: the amount of time you spend with colleagues can easily be longer, and more intense, than the time you spend with your partner. You can become very close; you experience lots of challenges together. Respect, a liking, and love can grow between people who have the chance to get to know each other over a long time, but who may not have been initially attracted to each other. If you are working in an already stressful work-place, it may be especially good to have a close person to discuss these pressures, who understands more, perhaps, than the person waiting for you at home.

The boss, in particular, is exposed to this, because in many organisations he is isolated, makes all the ultimate decisions, takes responsibility for the finances, recruitment, discipline, and so on, often with no one with whom to discuss and weigh up his actions. So when these isolated individuals find themselves working alongside someone they are attracted to, and with whom they can potentially discuss the grinding day-to-day issues they have to face, it can be a stimulating combination. All of a sudden, ideas can be shared and topics discussed with a person who knows all the players involved, is aware of the politics, and may even be in a position to help.

Given the boss's power to promote and reward, it is tempting for them, to a greater or lesser degree, to manipulate the people around them, to use their charisma, in order to get close to them, both physically and emotionally.

---

4. Although beyond the remit of this book, the Equal Opportunities Commission website offers a good starting point. www.eoc.org.uk. Note that they acknowledge that this is a form of bullying. In the US, see www.dol.gov; in Australia, www.hreoc.gov.au; in Canada, www.equalopportunity.on.ca.

"My wife doesn't understand me ..."

If the boss is married and tells you not to be concerned because "it's all over ...", please proceed with caution. If you are even partially attracted because they are 'the boss', have the flashy car, big salary or the power, then step back and get some distance on this. I have seen managing directors sobbing their eyes out like little kids as they suffer the trauma of managing the love triangle of their own creation. The chances are that the impact of the stress of trying to have an affair with you and get out of the marriage, while still trying to run a company, will mean he probably won't hold his boss position for much longer. Given the track record of divorce lawyers, the material goods will evaporate in fees. Will you still feel the same about this Love God when he's filling shelves in the local supermarket and getting the bus home? This may be a mean tactic, but I am trying to save you heartbreak!

Having said that, it is always possible that true love conquers all. But true love is more than the distractingly heady atmosphere of spending two nights in a distant four-star hotel with mini-bar, attending a conference.

The boss is having an affair ...

The *Boss In Love* may not be chasing you, but is having an affair with someone else, in or out of the office, and wants to use you to cover the lies he is telling his partner. What do you do then? There may be genuine reasons or undisclosed issues that mean the people involved end up 'playing away', shall we say, but to enlist the assistance of staff, especially in this case of a very young employee was wrong.

I saw this situation occur when my friend Alice started her first job. The MD was having an affair with a woman in the office and exploited my friend's inexperience and immaturity. Alice was keen to do well, but was too young to realise how he was taking advantage of her. He would arrive back from lunch, a little dishevelled, closely followed by the woman in question, who would actually look fine, but through the constant, nervous, unnecessary readjustment of her clothing, unwittingly gave the game away.

The MD would ask my friend to answer calls that were put through from his wife. He would ask her to tell his wife that he was out of the office or that he would be late home.

Alice remembers how she felt about this:

> *"It was my first job and I was completely unprepared for what was going on. I just didn't have a reference point against which I could check how I should behave. If, like everyone else in the office, I had just been an observer, it may have been tolerable, but things went beyond this.*
>
> *"I was so young that the situation that developed was more akin to abuse than any sort of manager/employee relationship. If I had been older and wiser, I would have had a few ideas of how to deal with it. As it was, I was unwillingly dragged in and became a collaborator in their affair. I think he was about 35. He managed our department of about ten. It was an open-plan office with the desks arranged in small groups. It was impossible not to hear other people's conversations, so we could all hear him talking to the woman and making arrangements to meet her. The 'lady' in question worked in an office in another part of the building. I did realise these things sometimes happened but I was upset when he asked me to lie for him. I started to dread going to work."*

You might think that having a boss who is having an affair would put you in a very strong position. Isn't he going to have to keep you on side? Isn't he concerned that you may tell someone and make life difficult for him with either his spouse or even his bosses? Won't he need to make life very pleasant for you at work, in an attempt to buy your goodwill?

If you are the sort of character who feels comfortable in being able to exploit this position, then good luck to you. In my experience, as with anyone who has an affair with the boss, you must be prepared that colleagues and other managers will take a very dim view of this behaviour and that you will suffer the fallout when the boss is inevitably exposed, fired, or moves on. It's a very risky game.

Alice didn't feel as though she had any control of the situation. Fielding his wife's calls made her feel very uncomfortable; if her boss did anything that singled her out or showed any favouritism, she felt embarrassed. She was worried about what her colleagues thought, but was not strong enough to do anything about it. Essentially, she did not know how to manage the situation. It was only when the woman involved moved to another company that her misery finally ended. There was no longer any need for Alice to be involved.

It's another situation where you should follow your gut instinct. It seems wrong, so it probably is wrong. Alice was not the person who needed to justify their behaviour.

If you know someone having this experience or are going through it yourself, there are lots of things you can do. First of all, find a colleague who will help you. A conversation with any senior manager who will take a very serious view of this sort of behaviour will ensure that you are released from this at the earliest stages.

It is an example of being afraid to do the right thing because of the fear of the consequences. If she had made a fuss, would her boss really have been able to afford to cause more trouble by making her life difficult in other ways? Unlikely. He's the bully, tell on him.

Secondly, ignore his requests as you would the name-calling of the *Fear Merchant* and enlist the support of colleagues like those in *No Power* boss.

Managing the *Boss In Love*

Summmary

There are a bunch of strategies you can employ which will be effective and limit the damage you may fear, and are certainly an improvement on remaining in 'victim status':

- Resist getting involved
  - ◆ No discussion, DON'T GET INVOLVED!
  - ◆ Whatever they threaten they have no right to ask
- Don't abuse the situation for personal benefit – it's a risky path
  - ◆ In refusing to be involved you are in the right, don't be afraid
- Share the information with a more senior colleague, (possibly anonymously) – it's behaviour that could affect the results of the company/department/team

Chapter Thirteen
Interviews

The truth about interviews

Getting the right person for the job is expensive. Even if a company does not pay a recruitment consultancy to find and hire you, the process of hiring staff involves huge cost. Many of these costs are fixed:

- The role needs to be advertised.

- Someone at the hiring company has to review the applications.

- Interviews have to be scheduled.

- The interview itself may take anything from 30 minutes to several hours over several meetings.

- Removing managers from their work to do the interviewing is one of the most costly expenses.

- Administration of the process, letters, calls and in some cases travel expenses mean that you, from the day you start, have a value. Your desk, computer, tools, equipment, phone, uniform, vehicle – all need to be ready for you when you start. The company does not want to go through this process again unnecessarily!

There are also other intangible costs. When a manager or a company offers you the post, they have to some extent put their reputation on the line. They are saying, in effect, "We think this is the right person for the job." If they are wrong, it will reflect badly on how their decision-making abilities are judged. Managers who make continuous errors of judgment in recruitment do not last long.

The company also invests in you emotionally. They want you to succeed; their success depends on it. From small family firms right up to large corporations, having invested time, money and manpower in hiring you, they want to recoup their costs and more! They hang their hopes on you; their success depends on your ability to deliver. Have they made the right deci-sion?

In other words, you have the greatest value the day you walk in the door. There is no need to be nervous on your first day. Let them make the fuss of you that you deserve. It may be hard to grasp that you don't have to impress them on the first day, let them impress you. The more relaxed you are, the more of the information that is being fed to you, you will remem-ber. You'll also appear more professional, and the respect this will earn you is invaluable.

First day summary

- Be calm – you will learn and remember more.
- Remember they paid for you, they have invested in you, their hopes are pinned on you.
- The impression you give in these early days could affect the rest of you time with that company.

What to find out at the interview

I regret not thinking this through thoroughly when I was working in recruitment. I did tell people not to try too hard at interview, on the grounds that if you were not being yourself, it was unlikely that you would be able to maintain any kind of false persona, and the fact that you thought it necessary to be 'someone else' suggested that you were probably not right for the job. But there is more you need to know.

When did you last go for an interview? Did you think about the personality of the person who would ultimately be your manager? Did you get the chance to meet them during the process? Some large corporations have an interview process that starts with the HR department or an outsourced hiring consultancy. Assuming you did meet your potential new boss, what did you ask them?

I used to advise people to learn as much as they could about the company, the growth strategy, the opportunity in their market and other wider company issues. I think I missed a trick. With the benefit of hindsight, I would now advise – especially if you have, or have had a mad boss – that you include the following as you interview them.

First of all, look at the person carefully and consider:

■ Are there any signs of their likely personality traits? Does he look stressed? Bitten-down nails can be a sign of a stressed, tense person, dark rings under the eyes might suggest working late hours.

■ Check out not just body language but look for a tired face. Does the person look overworked?

■ Does the boss look you in the eye? Or are the eyes constantly wandering?

■ Does he smile? Genuinely, that is.

■ Look at his clothes: smart or dishevelled? Have they made any effort for the meeting? If they are as successful as they claim, do the clothes match the story?

■ Does this boss listen attentively to what you have to say, or do they spend the interview telling you about their successes?

■ Does he answer your questions clearly?

■ Does he rush you? Does he try to finish sentences for you?

Your overall aim here is to assess whether what they say and the impression they give are congruent. Does the story add up? Because you need to know if working with or for this person is going to be a pleasant experience or not, because you are potentially committing yourself to spending many waking hours with them.

You can also pick up useful information about the company itself and the culture it promotes. For example, how were you treated when you arrived at reception? And how was the business of the interview conducted?

■ Do they start on time?

■ Do they engage in digressions?

186 IS YOUR BOSS MAD?

- Do other employees interrupt the meeting?
- Have all mobile phones been turned off?

There are aspects of the history of this job that will not have been published, so you need to find out:

- What happened to any predecessor?
  - Why did the predecessor leave?
  - Why did they fail?
- Why are they hiring now?
- Will he allow you to meet other employees without him?

Instead of just being nervous or excited about the interview and the prospect of a new job, I advise that you critically and carefully observe this person, and imagine, "If he or she is like this now, what will they be like to work with on a day-to-day basis?" Think about asking questions that challenge the conventions of interviewing.

The questions

- What qualities do you think the organisation recognised in you, when choosing you for promotion?
- How long have you been a manager?
- What do you feel are your best qualities, as a manager?
- Have you had any management training?
- What training (or further training) do you think would be beneficial?
- What attracted you to this company?
- What aspects of this company do you find most attractive/most restricting?
- Where do you see yourself in five year's time? (Yes, go on. Ask this one. After all, it's one they always ask you. You never know, you may get a sensible answer!)
- Does he know what's meant by succession planning? (Believe me, some don't!)

■ Does he have a review process?

■ Does that process encompass a 360 review?

The '360' means that all employees, including the boss, are reviewed from all angles, that is, by a colleague at the same level, by their manager, and by someone who reports to them. (Some companies additionally ask customers who interface with the employee, as well.) This method offers the chance to have a formal process for communicating any notable discord in their style. Note that companies who routinely perform 360s are likely to be more enlightened, and to have other innovative policies in place, such as stress risk assessment, buddy programmes (someone who looks after you carefully for the first three to six months) and formalised induction and training.

These questions are essential in trying to assess your new boss. Is there a chance they won't answer? It will, to some extent, depend not on what you ask but how you ask it. Be genuinely curious. Of course, there is a risk you will look like a smart-arse, but you should be able to get away with two or three of these.

It may shock them to be asked these questions, so play it by ear as to how many you decide to ask. You can soften these questions, there is no need to be blunt and direct. Ask them to describe their management style – many will never have formulated this in their minds before. Be OK with the silence while they are thinking – the answer will be worth waiting for.

It would be great if asking these questions became standard practice. Bosses should be absolutely prepared to respond. Interviews should be a truly two-way process.

Interview techniques

The negative interview

This interview starts like a conventional meeting. You will be asked general questions about your background, about what you want to achieve, your work skills. Then the interviewer describes a situation which is based on a typical problem you might be likely to encounter in the role. They could use a similar example to that which Jack encountered in chapter nine, where he was challenged on possible events at an ever-increasing level of complexity. It doesn't matter that you have a solution to any one problem, there is always some further hypothetical additional problem that cannot be resolved.

Because this is all make-believe (not based on your actual experience), there must come a time when you are unable to answer with anything constructive. How you feel and how this manifests at this stage is what matters to the interviewer. They want to see what happens to you when you are stressed, to assess at what point you give up. How determined are you? How inventive are your solutions? Do you at any point lose your temper? However, as I said before, this is probably not a particularly fair way of assessing people, especially if you recognise that it is a game. But if you are not aware that this is a 'technique' you can easily end up thinking that you have missed the point, or are being obtuse, but not understand why. But now you know. Fair enough, forewarned is forearmed. Knowledge is power ...

The 'stressovoye'

I just encountered some variations of the negative interview which aim to push you to your limit. Apparently such techniques are particularly popular in Eastern Europe. The interview starts normally with questions about your background and skills, and so on, but for no apparent reason the atmosphere of the meeting suddenly changes. The interviewer suddenly starts shouting at the candidate, accuses them of lying about their résumé and experience. They insult the person and ask intimate personal questions. There are even reports of candidates being told they can have the job if they are prepared to undergo plastic surgery. Sometimes they demand that the candidate leaves immediately and, in some cases, a glass of water is thrown in the face of the candidate.

The companies using these unconventional methods state that it helps them to assess candidates more accurately. They believe that a candidate who reacts aggressively to having the water thrown on them has strength of character and is exhibiting leadership qualities. Those who accept the humiliation and fail to react are seen as submissive and lacking in ambition. Which suggests that by using this strategy, only very aggressive people will end up in management roles. If you think that acting exceedingly aggressively is a quality normally associated with good leadership, then God help the staff!

Clearly, you have to decide whether you would want to work within a company that chooses to interview people like this.

There are other 'dirty tricks' that they can play on newly appointed staff. One is to call those who have just joined the company with a bogus job offer from another company. If the employee shows interest he is fired for showing a lack of loyalty to the firm. A variation I came across was used by a company that had to make redundancies in its IT department. It also set a covert 'test' for the team. On different days each person was asked to do a piece of work that would take several hours to complete, just 15 minutes before they were due to leave. The candidates selected for redundancy were chosen based on how they reacted to this request.

Knowing of these ploys is useful should you ever find yourself in a similar situation. Decide: do you want to work for an organisation that will exploit your good nature, your vulnerability, or fear of losing the job? In this case, the company wanted to identify people too weak to resist the request. People they knew they could in future press into longer hours, at short notice, for no reward. Hmmm, nice, NOT!

Silent desk

Another variation on the negative interview is the silent desk technique. You may be on your own or part of a small group of candidates who are shown into an office where a person is sitting behind a desk. They might being looking at a PC or appear to be engrossed in some paperwork. When being shown into the office it is indicated that you sit in one of the chairs, facing the person on the other side of the desk.

The person behind the desk does not acknowledge you. The company is watching to see how long you put up with being ignored. What will you eventually do or say? Are you aggressive, or incredibly patient? If with other candidates, do you interact with them? I can't tell you how you are 'supposed' to react as it really depends on the qualities the company is seeking. With this type of interview, I personally would remain only a few minutes. If they wanted a submissive, patient person, then I would not be right for them anyway. So if you are ever faced with one of these situations (and you may not immediately realise exactly what is going on) then do what you genuinely feel comfortable with. If that's what they're looking for, then you could be the right person for the job.

"Come for a drink …"

Another scenario is the invitation to a social event. I have seen this used many times and it can be very slick. You attend an interview and it seems to go well. The meeting will have been timed for late in the afternoon, or just before lunch. As you are leaving, you get a seemingly casual invitation from the interviewer. "The guys are heading for the pub, would you like to come along, be a good chance to get to know us a little better?" You are so pleased, this must be sign that they really like you, so of course you accept.

This is a set-up. It's all by design. They don't want you to get to know them, they are going to check you out: your interpersonal skills, how you carry yourself, whether you are inclined to dance on the table after a glass of Pinot Grigio, or roll under the table after several bottles. In roles where you need to entertain clients, attend conferences, and similar events, companies need to know that you have the social skills to cope. So beware; whilst it is a good sign to be asked, this is definitely a part of your interview process.

For very senior roles, some companies take this part of someone's character very seriously. If you are going to be representing an international, multi-million dollar organisation, you must really excel in social situations. Candidates may even be asked to attend a two or three-day residential interview process to be 'assessed'. I have heard of the candidate being filmed while in the bar, at a time when they thought they were not under scrutiny. Remember this when you apply for that role as president or CEO of the company!

Customer care

Many companies, claim to be 'customer centric' or focused. One airline, truly taking this to heart, decided upon an interview technique that would ensure that even its pilots would have the qualities required to support this statement. The pilot applying for a position would arrive at the airline's HQ to be greeted by a charming receptionist. The receptionist would apologise that the interviews were running 15 minutes behind schedule. She would then offer them a coffee and a tour of the building. The pilot would be asked to accompany the receptionist to the kitchen area to get the coffee.

The receptionist was actually working undercover. Her job was to check how the pilot reacted to her. If they were irritated at the delay, declined to accompany the receptionist, not interested in the tour or were in any way rude or impolite to her, they would not be offered the job. Her report on the candidate would be taken into account in the hiring process. The company didn't want to hire people who were dismissive of a 'lowly' receptionist. They were not considered to have the qualities which would enable the company to fulfil its desire to be truly customer centric. The way that the pilot may have potentially communicated with their customers would have been a concern.

The moral of these examples is that you need to be aware that organisations are getting increasingly sophisticated in how they learn more about you than can be gleaned from a standard interview.

Tips

Time management

To look very professional and organised ask how long you have for the interview. Looking at your watch is a great way to break rapport (you may actually want to do this if you've decided that this company is not for you). Otherwise, if a clock is not in clear view and you want to maintain rapport, take your wrist watch off at the beginning and put it on the table/ desk in front of you where you can glance at it without anyone noticing.

After all, you want to make sure you have enough time to ask those crucial questions.

Less a boss, more a raconteur ... or it's all about me!

Some interviews are surprisingly unconventional. I have met bosses who seem to view the whole event as an opportunity to tell you about their outstanding career and generally try to impress you. In this case do not panic if they fail to ask you anything about yourself or you don't get the chance to ask any questions. Just nod and smile appreciatively and let them get on with it. Do not worry about this. Leave them to deliver their monologue. Do not under any circumstances risk messing things up by making the mistake of trying to impress them. Left to drivel on uninterrupted, they will report that you are charming and attentive and will recommend you for the job. Yes, they will.

For me, this was a stage of an interview process where I had finally got to meet the CEO. He was a lovely man, but wow, could he talk! I didn't utter more than three words during the hour-long meeting.

Consider this situation a lucky break. Instead of having a grilling about your experience, sitting in front of a boss who loves nothing more than the sound of his or her own voice is a piece of cake. Muse: how did they get the job ...? Personally I love meeting people who are very senior and very mediocre. It means there's hope for all of us, doesn't it?

Role playing

Some interviews require you to take part in a role play. This is normally at a second or subsequent meeting. You will be invited to 'meet the team', so several people will be attending. The first time I was so embarrassed ... It seemed so funny to see the manager allotting roles to the staff, everyone was taking it so seriously. On this subject my advice is fluffy, I'm afraid. I would advise you to just throw yourself into it, and have fun. In many situations enthusiasm may count for much more than content or previous job experience.

Interview coaching

Recruiters often coach candidates excessively to get them ready for the interview process. This is not necessarily a bad thing, but recognise there are different agendas at stake here. They want to present the best possible person to the hiring company, they want to make the sale. It's got to be worth their while teaching you, parrot-like, some of the required responses to increase their chances of success.

However, I would caution against too much coaching for an interview, for all the reasons covered in this book! For one, you are so busy focusing on yourself, trying to get everything 'right', that you miss the telltale signs of the mad stressed boss and fail to ask the key questions you need answered. Secondly, if you are not truly right for the role you are setting yourself up for disaster. Don't try too hard. Be yourself, let them see you as you really are and accept you like that, not for what you imagine they want. If I were considering a list of golden rules that would certainly feature.

Your curriculum vitae or résumé

Fashions in CV-writing come and go, and numerous books, magazine and newspaper articles are continually being written about how best to present yourself in this rather odd document. Because of the many schools of thought about what it should look like it is almost impossible to please all the people all of the time. Some people like to write reams, but for most people two pages of information is enough. Personally, I wouldn't use a photograph on a CV, it can have as much negative as positive effect. Build the information as an inverted pyramid. In other words, put the information about your most recent experience at the top, tailing off to your more distant less relevant experience. Personal details are fine, but no employer needs to know your partner is aged 42 or that your 12-year-old twins are called Barry and Larry. Less is more, so they say …

Again though, it is similar to the interview. Although it is a good thing to be professional, present the document as you would yourself in a smart and positive way (check spelling, avoid gaps in work history, or have good reasons for them, use a simple font, stick to the facts) it is still a reflection of you, how you work and what you are like. Trying too hard to please an (unknown) audience may not pay off. You don't know their particular preferences or style, so be yourself and the chances of getting the right match in a boss will increase.

Set up for success

Whatever job you choose to do, carefully consider all the consequences. Some people take a new position without fully thinking through the implications of its location or other non-employer related issues. For example, do you really want a job which entails an exhaustingly long commuting journey? If you are bringing up a young family then it's probably best not to agree to work abroad if you have to leave them behind.

Set realistic and manageable goals. And if you're not getting what you want, be prepared to walk away. There's always something better, more appropriate for you as long as you keep on looking. Don't let your life become a continuous struggle, so much so that you find yourself in a depressed state, which you yourself have created, but could have avoided, and then wonder why …

Chapter Fourteen
Stress

Where to get help

- First, what does stress look like?
- How do you know you are suffering stress?
- What are the typical symptoms of work-related stress?

Here is a list of symptoms gathered from private healthcare companies and the HSE (Health and Safety Executive) I guess you may already know what the signs are and what is causing it but this list does show the wide number of different ways it could affect you, and no doubt affects different people in different ways.

How to recognise stress

The symptoms manifest as both physical and mental problems

Physical symptoms:

- increased susceptibility to colds and other infections
- headaches
- muscular tension
- backache and neckache
- excessive tiredness
- difficulty sleeping
- digestive problems
- raised heart rate

- increased sweating
- lower sex drive
- skin rashes
- blurred vision

Emotional and behavioural changes:

- wanting to cry much of the time
- feeling that you can't cope
- short temperedness at work and at home
- feeling that you've achieved nothing at the end of the day
- eating when you're not hungry
- losing your appetite
- smoking and drinking to get you through the day
- inability to plan, concentrate and control work
- getting less work done
- poor relationships with colleagues or clients
- loss of motivation and commitment

If you decide you are stressed from work, whom do you turn to? How can you tell if it's because you are really under a lot of pressure, are unhappy with your job, or if it's 'just you'?

The first step is to tell someone about your feelings. You could start with your family and friends. However, this may not be very helpful as you are the person having the experience first-hand, and even loved ones may not understand what you are going through. In the past you may have protected them from truth about your role, and their response may be, "Why are you complaining now?"

You can approach someone in your company's personnel or HR department, but this isn't always a good route either. The management may have a hidden agenda. (For example, if you get given a task to do 15 minutes before you are due to leave, get suspicious – see page 189) You should be able to tell from how others have fared and by what policies are already in place, what sort of reception your problem receives. Enlightened organisations which have a stress risk assessment policy in place should be most understanding.

If you don't have the luxury of these people or policies and departments, whom do you turn to then? Colleagues? They may be sympathetic but unlikely to be able to help practically. Your boss? Even if he is not directly causing the stress, he may be the person responsible for implementing a stressful process. Despite being sympathetic, he may not be able to change anything. Actually, there is always a risk in telling your boss you are stressed. Without any formalised processes in place, management may turn around your reasons for claiming stress and accuse you of not being up to the job. If it's mad boss you are dealing with, then you certainly will have a big problem on your hands.

What about your boss's boss? If you are feeling stressed and under pressure, this may be a difficult thing to do. So you might turn to the big recognised organisations that are there to help, and fight your cause, aren't they?

Almost all work stress is caused by poor management. Now let me explain that …

Poor management may manifest itself as anything from a snotty shop girl, having been promoted to manageress, throwing her weight around and upsetting staff, to a project management team designing a *profitable* process for a 700-seat call centre, which means they can make more money by cutting the morning tea break from the agents' daily routine. Track back: who was responsible for promoting the shop girl? Who said a distant project team should be allowed to control the day of the call centre worker in such a detailed, yet detached, way?

To avoid stress you need to set things up that ensure success. Have you got the right tools for your work, the right training, and necessary support? Is the amount of work you need to do clearly communicated?

Stress from processes

If you complain that it is difficult customers causing your work stress then change the service or product you are delivering. It's actually part of your system that is causing a problem to the customer; the answer will be to investigate and rectify it, but for this you will need to convince the boss. They may be the person who designed or agreed the process. Formulate and communicate your rationale for changes with facts to back up the suggestions, and with calmness.

Stress from working conditions

If you complain about poor or difficult working conditions causing you stress at work, then it is once more the responsibility of your managers to sort out these problems. Their lack of attention to any working conditions that are creating stress must be questioned and possibly shared with outside authorities.

Mobile phones in the workplace

This is a true story, which illustrates the behaviour of a person so stressed by their job, they have lost the normal boundaries. I once called the PA of an executive to arrange meeting. She answered her mobile phone, which had been diverted from her landline. It was obvious from the echo on the call that she was not at her desk, but she said she would call me back to confirm the time I had requested. Fifteen minutes later she called me back. 'I'm sorry I couldn't confirm the time earlier' she apologised 'but I was in the ladies'.

Yeeeuch! Right, OK, this is another potential golden rule. Don't answer your phone in the toilet, EVER! Don't even take it with you! You have the right to some privacy. It's appalling, DON'T DO IT! Callers can leave a message; you can call back. No role should be putting you under so much pressure that this tiny amount of personal time and attention should be lost. Now, promise me you won't …

Responsibility

There are some circumstances in which the management is not ultimately responsible for work stress.

Most people have some control over the job they choose, and will not engage in something they know would be beyond their personal stress tolerance. For example, don't work in an abattoir if you are a vegetarian, don't apply to a nursery if you don't like kids, and so on. Once you have chosen a job that avoids your personal stress triggers, and provides the tools, the environment, and the training you need, then the only remaining variable is the people you work with and for. In summary, everything can be in place, but if the managers are poor, your choice and the environment will count for nothing.

Either through error or design, the boss or the management dictate the stress level of your job. Yet thanks to the advice of many of the organisations you might approach for help, they are somewhat 'let off the hook' as the advice they offer, more often than not, deflects the responsibility of the stress away from the organisation or your manager towards issues that were probably caused by them! For example, if they blame your inability to cope at work because of 'relationship issues', they are taking an assumptive view that the relationship issues came first, and not that they could possibly have been fuelled by the problems you have at work.

Whilst these organisations accept and state that, "Most work-related stress is related to management of work, relationships at work, organisational set-up and whether you feel you have power and control in your work" (a quote from a major private healthcare company), unfortunately, the solutions they offer are unworkable.

The same private healthcare company also notes on its website that, "In the UK it is estimated that work-related stress is responsible for six million days of sick leave a year, with stress being linked to many minor and major illnesses."

I don't think it ungenerous to observe that it may not be in their interest to give advice that will really resolve your work stress issues, free, on the internet. *How* do they make their money?

If you seek advice and help with dealing with your stress it is frequently suggested by these organisations that you discuss the issue with your boss. This could prove very challenging with a mad boss.

Typically these organisations go on to offer helpful advice like this:

> *"If work-related stress is affecting you, it is important to deal with the problem as soon as possible. One of the most important factors in reducing stress levels is managing time effectively. Prioritise tasks, delegate where necessary and take care not to take on more than you can handle. Completing one task before going on to the next will help you to feel more in control of work, while varying tasks will help to keep you interested.*

> *"Make time to relax at work by stretching and breathing deeply. This will help you to keep focused and prevent tired muscles. Simply ensuring you get outside for a walk during your lunch break can be helpful."*

I am disappointed because it makes massive assumptions. It describes the workplace as offering freedom in self-management and choice of activity. If you have a workplace where you can 'delegate', 'vary tasks', easily 'manage time' or even escape to get a lunch break, it probably isn't a place that would cause a high level of stress, thus the 'advice' loses credibility. By choosing an irrelevant example, they are completely ignoring any relevant culture issues.

Choosing your level of stress

Another leading private healthcare organisation's website advises people who are asking for help because they have 'work-related stress': "You may feel stress from work. Visit the doctor. He may prescribe antidepressants." This is word for word their insightful advice! Well, I guess they are selling drugs …

What does that really solve? It's like covering a broken arm with a Band-Aid; the problem hasn't gone away nor have you dealt with the underlying situation.

You need to treat the cause not the symptom. Here the cause is the management, your boss. Try and learn behaviours, language and thought processes that relieve the problem. Unless you learn from your experiences, potentially you could go from job to job, suffering from a string of bullies and from pressure you cannot handle. Understand the way your brain is processing the information and turn around the way you deal with it. If you don't do this, you will end up with two problems: the work issues stay unresolved and you are now taking prescription drugs!

This is tantamount to a medical crime. You now not only have the problem at work, you are dependent on drugs to deal with it. Hey, that's really gonna help your performance. Thank you private healthcare!

If you are suffering from stress, then you need to deal with the underlying causes of it, not the symptoms. And that means starting with the situation.

The website continues with more staggering ways to resolve that stress!

Lifestyle changes

"Regular activities outside work will help you to meet new people, take your mind away from work worries and remind you that there is more to life than the office. Bring a sense of fun into your life by starting a new hobby."

Give me strength! Start a new hobby? That's bound to solve everything! What with the antidepressants supplied by the GP to solve your *work-*

related stress, I can see you spaced out of your brain on prescription drugs, playing with your set of shiny new golf clubs …

Until every people-manager is trained, every workplace has a stress risk assessment policy (and follows it!), and every company recognises the real value of happy employees, the advice that these organisations offer should include practical techniques for coping with the bad boss environment. It would also be helpful to recognise that the culture of your company and the personality of your boss could also be causing the problem. There is no point in getting people to engage in activities or prescribing drugs that distract them, but which will not change the underlying cause of the stress.

Stress and anger

There is little to be gained from losing your temper at work, with either your boss or your colleagues. Anger is very powerful, but don't let it control you, especially in the workplace, as most of the time you will end up suffering. Being able to keep calm when people all around are losing their cool gives a very powerful message to others. And, as with building confidence, the more you do this, the easier it becomes each time you are tested.

Use any angry feelings to give you energy. In the work situation, be motivated to do something about the problem that's causing the anger. Get to the bottom of things, rather than venting your spleen on whoever is around at the time. It is through communicating, gathering information, being curious, that you develop your own leadership potential. Every moment of conflict can be part of building the foundations for being a future 'sane' boss.

If you have decided that a particular boss or company is not for you, then make sure that you see this decision in a positive light, because at the next interview it is almost certain you will be asked why you left that job. And you certainly don't want to have your old boss refuse to give you a reference or only provide a bad one, or suggest that you were a 'troublemaker'. You are the winner if you can come away intact with nothing potentially coming back to haunt you.

Whenever you do leave a job, be in control. Don't get mad; there is no need to fall out with people. Nor is it about getting even. Thinking in terms of this kind of polarity limits your options. Once the momentary pleasure of humiliating an ex-boss or colleague has passed, it will seem a bitter pill when a new role slips from your grasp because you are rejected on the basis of damaging information from your past.

Even if you feel like writing a note telling that guy you sat next to for the last three years that you hated his scratching, and that he smells – don't! He might be a contact for some future requirement. He may be the right person for something you need, or he may need a job himself and you know someone who might want him. When you leave, say good-bye, make sure you have a note of everyone's contact details – telephone number, email address – and occasionally be in touch. Very easy, very civilised and potentially very useful. Once you have departed, your relationship with your now ex-boss changes dramatically. You are free of him; you can speak to him in a completely different way. Make him a part of your network.

You never know how people, positions or organisations are going to change. Roles change, and the most unexpected people end up in powerful, decision-making positions. And remember that you are also potentially part of everyone else's networks, and that you will be contacted out of the blue when someone has a job for you, when they need help, advice, information or just to say hello. The network is useful because you never know when you might need someone's help.

Although you are putting a value on this particularly challenging role, this is only your current impression. Life is unpredictable, perceptions are fickle, everything changes … This is not wishy-washy thinking. Whatever happens, you need to be paying attention, looking for opportunities, keeping your future options open. You only do that by stepping back from time to time to notice the bigger picture, and to reframe events to tie in with your growing professional reputation. Sure, it's enlightened self-interest, but this is the game, and part of your game plan is about staying in control.

Dealing with stress

Suggesting that you speak to your manager about work-related stress is not unreasonable advice, but it could mean that you are actually approaching the person who is the source of that stress. If that is the case, then you first need some advice on how to do this without actually increasing the stress!

I know I was rather dismissive about advising people to take up a hobby as a cure for work-related stress. It is actually quite important to engage in some skill or activity that is not related to work. Playing a tough sport, doing voluntary work or using any skill that increases your personal confidence will help you cope better with a stressful job. It may even mean you grow the confidence you need to help you solve the problem.

Chapter Fifteen
Fun Stuff

You mean, work can be fun?

Once upon a time your mad boss heard at a far distant conference or meeting at head office that happy staff means happy customers, and that there was a correlation between happy customers and financial reward for the company. But now, this is no more than a distant, hazy memory. So if you want to start transforming your workplace then it's up to you to remind him. If you need to convince him with the sort of communication he might recognise, use a diagram like the one below. It's the first step. If you search the internet, you'll find any number of formal and anecdotal reports on the link between happy staff and happy customers.

Linking Employee Satisfaction, Customer Satisfaction and Business Results

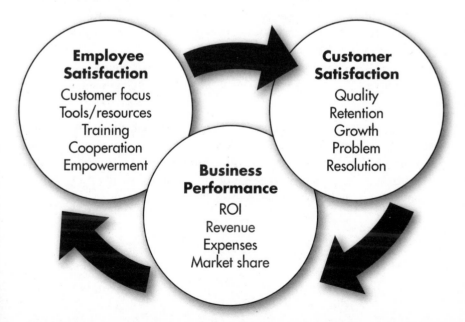

If you want to change your workplace, start by bringing some fun to work.

Is your boss mad? Is he going to embrace your desire or be a real old misery about it?

Although I can suggest many ways to introduce a little levity to your workplace, if the boss is not in the mood, you may find you're wasting your time. So you need a two-pronged strategy.

First, make sure your suggestions are welcome. Secondly, introduce the fun in ways that ensure success so that more events can be planned. I know there is nothing stopping you from organising your own get-togethers outside of work, but the object here is to get everyone in your office, shop, department, or team involved. Social gatherings outside of work are by definition social, not everyone is invited, the company may not contribute, and the boss not be exposed to the benefits of 'team-building'.

All the ideas set out below are deliberately fairly low key and low cost. If you are with a company that's prepared to shut down and take all the staff to the beach for the day, you may not need this chapter. Though that may not be the case. I have come across examples of companies with poor cultures, from a working perspective, which use a 'big splash' day out as a way to create the illusion of a healthy culture. Does one day out, however much money they have been prepared to spend, affect or improve the day-to-day life of the employee? If it's back to the grindstone the following day, what has been the real value? Is it just the company easing its guilty conscience?

I am suggesting these activities for companies that have lost their way; where the intensity of work pressure has meant the evaporation of any communication between staff, except that of work-related topics, and where even a small break in the monotony and routine will bring motivational benefits that far outweigh the small cost.

What's in it for the boss? How do you convince him?

Like all human beings, he will like any idea that makes him look good. He will like any ideas that improve results, be they financial or operational. Can he deliver some good outcome of a fun event to his boss?

These are the questions and issues you should bear in mind when formulating your plans.

■ What are your objectives? What are you asking him, or the company to contribute? Time, money, venue?

■ Create a plan – it doesn't have to be too formal – identifying what you want to do, what you need, if anything, from the company and what you think the benefits will be.

Here is one of the most simple and effective activities I have experienced which I hope will be workable in your environment:

"Hey, it's picnic day!"

You are going to hold a company (or department, team, or section) picnic. The difference is, this picnic is held at the workplace. It's a good way of introducing new people to the company or of broadcasting news. The idea is to get everyone together at one time. Instead of people going off for lunch at different times, lay on a picnic at the workplace. For the boss you can suggest that it will be a good opportunity for him to deliver any (brief) announcements. He may like the idea of having a platform and, for the mad boss, having the experience of doing something boss-like, such as taking on the role of and behaving like a real leader. That would be a positive activity for all present.

The 'rules':

■ You ask your boss to pay for the food.

■ You may need to discuss the appropriate area to hold the picnic. Can it be in the department/office, or should it be in a staff rest area or meeting room?

■ As everyone is to be included, you will need to arrange cover for phone calls and other ongoing external interruptions.

- Ask the boss to announce, or say something to the effect, "Thanks for coming, I hope you enjoy this. We'll have another one in a month's time" and so on.

What's in it for the boss?

- He can use it for communicating: "Here are the latest results. This is the challenge this month" and so on.
- Everyone hears the same message at the same time.
- The boss gets to meet the new staff informally.
- The boss can tell everyone about other 'fun' events that will be starting (see the ideas to come).
- The staff are motivated. It is enjoyable to relax for a while with colleagues.

What's in it for the staff?

- Free food. (You mean, there is such a thing as a free lunch? Well, not exactly … there are conditions attached.)
- Speaking to people that you might not normally talk to in your workplace.
- Hearing company news.
- Having the chance to ask questions about that news.
- Telling everyone your news.
- Meeting new colleagues.
- A break from routine.
- Hear about the planned, future fun events.
- Interact with the boss in a more relaxed atmosphere.

If the company already boasts a canteen, just make sure that everyone invited to the picnic is there at the same time by holding a specific 'event'. You may need to arrange for a particular type of food to be served, or you may want to section off an area for your team/department meeting, and possibly decorate it in a specific style (with a minimal budget). How about mocking up a fake VIP style 'are you on the guest list?' event … Oh come on – it's supposed to be fun!

This may seem pretty 'small potatoes', but it's a good starting point. If you haven't done it before you'll soon realise how useful the team picnic becomes and how much everyone enjoys it. Just imagine getting *Mr Long Hours* out of his shell for this, or grabbing a few moments of lucid *Friend Then Foe Then Friend Again* boss.

Still no?

Bosses who are very mad and bad will probably not agree to even a small event like this. You still want to improve the atmosphere in the workplace, so you really need to sell the benefits of having some fun events, so make him an offer.

Companies have targets. What target could your team agree to meet that would make the picnic a suitable reward? Make sure it's highly achievable, of course. Here I have to hand this challenge over to you. Whatever you arrange should be a good way to kick off this process, with the boss seeing immediately the positive effect of a motivational event.

Remember the earlier strategies in the book. If you have bothered to put together some sort of plan suggesting a fun motivational event that is subsequently rejected, resubmit it to you boss's boss. I realise this is not likely to improve relations, but it exposes the rejection of your great ideas by your manager. It also highlights your innovative and embracing concern for the well-being of your colleagues and the success of the company. So you are reinforcing the potential benefits to all. Hmm. That sounds like great leadership to me …

Good luck!

More fun event ideas

"Who is that baby?"

An old favourite that always brings a laugh to the workplace is the baby picture competition.

You only need the boss to agree to display the pictures. He doesn't actually have to do anything, but even if he agrees but does not submit a picture, I can guarantee he will not be able to resist a sneaky look at the pictures, maybe when everyone has left. Perhaps you can persuade him to provide prizes? Or to be the judge? It will be excellent if you can get him to participate. With your mad boss, so many of the things you will be trying to do happen with baby steps like this.

Ask everyone to bring in a picture of themselves taken before they were 18 months old. Display the pictures without revealing who is who. The idea is to get everyone to guess which picture belongs to whom.

You may have prizes for different categories (prettiest baby, most recognisable face, and so on) or for the person who gets the most right. This game can last up to a week. Set up the pictures on a Monday, competition answers gathered through the week with results and prize giving on Friday.

It's so simple, very low cost, you could even have a small entry fee with the money raised going to a charity. The possibilities are endless …

This is purely for fun, if will break the routine even if it doesn't reinvent the culture.

Build a team from the team …

This may mean some out of work activity but will still fulfil the purpose of being motivational, fun and bringing people in your workplace closer.

The idea is to build a team from within your department or section, whom everyone can follow and support. Examples would be: a five-a-side football team, a darts team, a ballroom dancing team, a synchronised swimming team, and so on. Finding out everyone's 'hidden' skills will be a real eye-opener for a start. You'll be surprised.

If the team gets involved with the local community it may attract some attention. Would the boss enjoy the attention this might bring to his business? What will he contribute for this 'free' publicity?

If you are part of a big company, are there enough people for interdivisional competition?

What's in it for the boss?

■ Raising his own and the company's profile locally

■ If part of a bigger organisation raising the profile of the department/division manager within the company

■ Improving team spirit and motivation

■ Something to announce at the company picnic

■ Potential for publicity for the business

■ Limited impact on 'company time'

What's in it for the staff?

■ Enjoyment of supporting your team

■ Social, motivational, and stress reducing!

■ May persuade boss to contribute, time, money rewards

■ Chance to combine a sport/pursuit with work

"It's for charity"

Ask the boss to help you support a charity event. There are numerous angles to this: it could be a local or a nationwide charity event. It could be connected to an employee. Again, discovering people's concerns and interests builds strong relationships, which are useful when deadlines and projects in the workplace need to be completed by a team.

As well as actually taking part in the event, you can have fun arranging sponsorship. Can you arrange for everyone to sponsor Terry in accounts for jumping out of a plane? The more people involved the better.

Any objections from the boss about taking work time for publicising the event, collecting of forms, money, and so forth, may be countered by reminding him of the likely favourable publicity that will follow.

"Is that comfortable?"

Have you ever noticed how readily some men, with minimal persuasion, will jump at the opportunity to put on women's clothing? I'm intrigued by the enthusiasm with which they don tights and lipstick in order to reveal something of their 'feminine' nature. It's honestly a mystery to me.

Now organising cross-dressing day at work may be a step too far, but how about a day where people don't look like they normally do? That could be fun:

- Dress down day could be weekly event
- Dress in the style of the sixties/seventies/eighties Day
- Dress older or younger – great for rummaging around in your teenager's or granny's wardrobe

Any of these could be hilarious, but you probably wouldn't want to do it on a weekly basis. But there are many other occasions – commemorations, sporting events which offer an excuse for fancy dress.

The benefits for all are:

- Laughter
- Break from routine
- Breaking down of barriers

Apart from a contribution for prizes, the cost is low. Where I have seen this sort of event in action, the effect is amazing.

So how would it be if people couldn't wait to get to work!

"You can't put that!" caption competition

Create a competition based around the characters in the team. Take pictures of your colleagues or your boss in the work situation, either natural or posed, which involve them doing something, talking to someone, using the photocopier – whatever! Set up the picture and ask people to think of a caption.

As an alternative, create a quote of the week, or a new mission statement. Use your creativity.

Customer participation

Is there any way you can involve your customers with your fun stuff? If you are in an environment which has a strong and immediate customer focus, such as in a restaurant, store or other service organisation, find a way to demonstrate the link between your efforts and having happy customers. Could you hold a party for your customers? (How about getting them to dress up!) How about asking them to join in the sponsorship? Will they attend such and such event? Once you start breaking down the traditional barriers, life becomes so much richer than skulking in a workplace where a mad boss rules with too much stick and not enough carrot …

These ideas are just some initial thoughts about the ways in which you could start chipping away at the culture created by your mad boss. Even arranging for everyone, including the boss, to have a meal one evening is better than nothing. But whatever you do, it has to be an invitation issued to everyone. There is little groundbreaking activity happening if it's just a bunch of work colleagues socialising together.

The keys to successfully challenging the negative culture of your work-place are to:

■ Keep re-emphasising the benefits

■ Produce the tangible evidence of the benefits

■ Remind the boss of the low cost and the minimal impact on the working day

■ Promote the correlation between happy employees and happy customers

■ Be prepared to trade – if you achieve target x will they give you y?

If you have ever walked into a shop or restaurant where the staff are buzz-ing, welcoming, smiling and happy you know how important happy staff are and what effect they can have on your experience of that business. You make a note to return there in future. The call centre agent who sounds positive and who really makes you feel like they want to help you ensures an enjoyable experience. What do customers who have had a good experience do? They tell everyone. Therefore, make sure your boss is clear about this link. How much money does a company think about spending on new corporate branding, an advertising campaign, or the adoption of an internal policy regarding 'customer centricity'? When the same results can be achieved from having empowered, motivated, happy employees, thinking in a different way ... Weigh up the relative costs.

Another part of this excellent 'win-win' (a somewhat cheesy corporate expression) is the positive press the happy workplace attracts. If your workplace becomes somewhere people aspire to work, there's even more financial benefit. Your boss will have the pick of the best people. They will have heard what a great place it is to work. The cost of advertising for staff and recruitment costs will plummet. Just as customers recommend a great business, employees will recommend a place to work. Remember to include these comments when submitting your fun event plans.

Happy employees:

- Stay longer – they create a knowledge base and minimise the cost of continuous training of new staff
- Recommend the employer
- React in a positive way with customers

Words of caution – the office party

What can I say? The office party or the Christmas event, they are all recipes for disaster. I did consider including a whole chapter just on company dos, they are such a minefield of activity. You have all the right ingredients. You have the mad boss, the disgruntled employees, and essentially – alcohol. Mix together liberally for a couple of hours and then stand back. I have heard of people actually fighting with the boss, and with each other. The mix of the non-workplace environment, the drinks, and the emotion all fuel the 'frank exchanges' that are not uncommon at these events.

But you definitely should attend. It can be the best gossip for weeks afterwards. Here are my tips:

■ Don't hit or kiss anyone, especially the boss

■ Don't drink too much

These two points are closely related; beyond this my job here has been to highlight the potential pitfalls of the office party, but as people who know me will testify, I am hardly that well qualified to be telling you what to do, but let's move on ...

Chapter Sixteen
Saying Goodbye

They made you laugh …

Mad bosses are not in any way 'ordinary'. They stand out in your memory: some bosses made you smile, some made you cry. With their behaviour, they become the stuff of legends. And they also said things that made you cringe, or laugh out loud – either with them at the time, or at them later.

What did he say? Mad boss expressions

It may require you to put a little time and space between a mad boss and the experience you've had with them but at some stage these memories will soften. With the benefit of distance, you will recall you mad boss's antics – and smile. Apart from the hassle, the frustration, the long hours, the abuse and the tears, there will have been times, I'm sure, when you look back at your mad boss, his behaviour and things he said, and laugh. It could have been his way of bashing the table so hard that it broke. Or the time he breathed in so deeply, preparing to shout, that the buttons burst off his shirt (that was a Peruvian boss …). Or it could have been the things he said to you which now, with the addition of hindsight, you cannot believe ever upset or annoyed you.

I am sure you will remember some expressions or comments that your mad boss used; how about these real examples I have collected.

- A sales manager example, I'm afraid. This chap was running a sales meeting and was trying to inject a little fun, but perhaps he was going a little too far, as at 8.30 on a Monday morning he handed out the masks to the confused team: "Look, just try and think like Princess Leia, I am going to be Darth Vader." At least he was trying …

- A manager advises a new starter to try their best, he wants them to try as hard as he once did: "I dipped my toe in, right up to my knees …" (And he was serious.)

And these don't even start to examine the jargon now common in the workplace, that so many of us enjoy. I would look into it now but I think we are already singing from the same hymn sheet, but thanks for running it up the flagpole, let's try and achieve a win-win situation, I am prepared to go the extra mile, and will try not to move the goalposts ... we must do lunch ...

Plane spotting

This is the story of a new managing director starting at a technology company with a global brand, whose office happened to be based under the flight path of London's Heathrow airport.

On his first day, the senior management team, in the luxurious boardroom, set out to deliver a series of presentations, earnestly explaining their roles, introducing the company, and generally communicating the challenges and targets they faced. But by lunchtime, the staff were distraught. This new guy was a tough cookie. He must be bored! He was constantly looking out of the window. What should they do? The presentations must be terrible. What should they be telling him?

After lunch as the new MD's disengaged behaviour continued, they finally cracked. "Sir" ventured the flustered operations director, mid way through delivering his spiel, "I can't help feeling that we might perhaps be on the wrong track today. What would you like to hear about, you are obviously not interested in what we've said so far?" The MD looked at him, dragging his eyes away from the window. "No, you're all right mate! God, I'm going to love working here, I just LOVE watching those planes ..."

I think I would have loved to have worked with this guy. I wonder how soon the team worked out he was a mad boss?

Goodbyes

You will have good and bad memories of all the people you have worked with and for, but after this exploration of the world of mad bosses it's time for our goodbyes, and not just my farewell to you, patient reader.

Goodbye (1)

You are saying goodbye to misconceptions that may have held you back or blinkered your decisions.

■ To the idea that, in this day and age, you are rewarded for your loyalty. Generally, you are not. Having many years of service with one company on your CV can be construed as showing a lack of ambition or drive. Familiarity can breed contempt and many organisations are guilty of this attitude towards their employees. When companies decide to downsize, it is the market forces, the interests of shareholders and money, that are uppermost in the organisations' thoughts; loyal workers are unlikely to be part of any decision. Place your loyalty carefully, where it will be appreciated.

■ To the idea that you can't change your mind or alter track. If you are not happy, change it. Stop worrying about what other people think. As we have explored in the previous chapters, your level of happiness, stress, boredom or any other feeling is exclusive to you. Just because it works for someone else, it isn't guaranteed to work for you.

■ To saying 'yes' if you believe that you have to say yes to everything people ask of you, then you really need to practise saying no instead. You will find it quite liberating as those previously assumed obligations and responsibilities are no longer your concern. Practise at first in situations where it's no big deal, and then work your way up to the pressurising demands. You will find that saying no is wonderful, powerful, and releasing – and many people do not say it often enough.

Goodbye (2)

You are going to say goodbye to being a victim. If you have been suffering under a mad boss, now it is going to stop. There are things to do, things to plan; it could become a busy time, engaging in all this positive activity. This is your life: you can't go on wasting any more time vaguely thinking that "it will all be different one day" because it won't unless you start putting energy into changing it. So why are you waiting?

You could get lucky and find employment that you feel comfortable with, or even love. But there is a chance that you might not. Increase your chances of success by taking action. The first step for you might be as easy as simply leaving this book in sight, on your desk, in the canteen, or carried under your arm ...

Goodbye (3)

Goodbye to your old lifestyle, to worries and old behaviours. Take a really deep breath, enjoy the prospect. Learn the advantages of perspective. Appreciate the wider picture in situations. You respond to multiple forces, emotions and agendas in your working life. By working out the real motivations behind these forces you can start controlling those you embrace and those you reject, and make calm decisions about how you react. Start to see what *really* matters.

Mad bosses will always be a part of our lives, so learn to recognise them, and treat them for what they are. Because that way you will be ensuring that your working life will be as happy as you can make it.

Are you going to enjoy work tomorrow?

Further Information

Contact me on:

jill@isyourbossmad.com

www.isyourbossmad.com

Index

A
Abuse 105, 133, 136, 168, 169, 180, 182, 217
Abused 124, 135, 142, 150, 153
Advertising 83, 130, 131, 132, 171, 214
Agent 84, 85, 197, 214
Aggression 2, 15, 18, 21, 43, 111, 138, 155, 159, 160
Aggressive 4, 11, 22, 31, 34, 36, 44, 45, 46, 49, 53, 108, 110, 113, 116, 121, 123, 131, 132, 139, 141, 145, 148, 149, 150, 155, 157, 158, 189
Alcohol 139, 214
Anger 18, 19, 20, 29, 52, 54, 65, 99, 105, 202
Antidepressants 200, 201
Are you a Boss 22
Assertive 44, 45
Assertiveness 24, 99

B
Best practice 47, 48
Bully 70, 76, 107, 108, 109, 110, 148, 150, 151, 181
Bullying 4, 12, 15, 21, 99, 100, 105–108, 152, 154, 177

C
Call centre 82–86, 197, 214
Change 12, 13, 21, 28, 29, 36, 40–43, 45, 47, 49, 56, 59, 63, 68, 70, 75, 76, 79, 87, 92, 99, 103, 108, 113, 119, 137, 153, 171, 197, 198, 202, 203, 206, 219
Charity 25, 26, 210, 211
Clique(s) 145, 147, 163, 168

Colleagues 5, 12, 24, 38, 51, 54–56, 63, 67, 70, 72, 76, 77, 85, 99, 102, 104–108, 110, 117–122, 132, 136, 139, 148, 150, 170, 173, 175, 178, 180, 181, 196, 197, 202, 208, 209, 212, 213
Communication 14, 18, 20, 24, 47, 48, 54, 91, 92, 118, 120, 121, 140, 150, 151, 205, 206
Company picnic 207
Competition 32, 138, 172, 210–212
Confidence 9, 18, 21, 36, 41, 42, 44, 56, 63, 70, 71, 79–81, 85, 108, 115, 118, 121, 125, 127, 139, 148, 202, 204
Control 13, 19, 20, 26, 41, 43, 49, 52, 53, 63, 65, 67, 68, 71, 72, 75, 76, 83, 86, 88–90, 108, 110, 119, 128, 142, 146–148, 151, 152, 166, 180, 196, 197, 199, 200, 202, 203
Culture 52, 60, 64, 66, 70, 72, 76, 152–154, 161, 169, 170, 173, 185, 200, 202, 206, 210, 213
Curriculum vitae (See also CV) 193
Customers 23, 35, 50, 69, 76, 81–85, 104, 105, 107, 108, 128, 136, 138–140, 143, 157, 167, 187, 191, 198, 205, 213, 214
CV (See also curriculum vitae) 9, 10, 13, 123, 153, 193, 219

D
Depression 15, 25, 148, 200–201
Discipline 17, 18, 24, 39, 99, 100, 105, 178
Discrimination 12, 148
Dismissal 12, 19, 70, 118, 127, 154, 155
Drivers 5, 10, 11, 13, 19, 40, 69
Duvet days 65